Ai IN 8 MINUTES

AI in 8 Minutes
by David Bruce

MJJP Consulting Ltd
Cambridge, United Kingdom
2025

Published in the United Kingdom.

Second edition, 2025

Author's note

This book aims to demystify some of the core concepts that underly artificial intelligence. We will explore them and discuss current applications of AI as well as look at future trends and the implications for us in the realms of travel, education and entertainment as well as look at what this means for us all in our work lives.

Each section of this book is designed to be read and understood in eight minutes or less. Some sections are longer as the concepts are move complex and require more explanation. As we will discover, AI is great at creating content, but not so great at understanding the ***context*** and ***meaning*** of what has been created. Especially when we are looking at more nuance and need to have a deeper understanding of how AI can really help us.

To that end this book has **not** been created using AI, except where specific details of AI tooling or AI examples are required. Even then, as we shall see, AI systems have an alarming predisposition to make stuff up, so where I have used AI, I have also checked with multiple other sources as well to confirm that the facts are indeed correct.

Since the first version was published in early 2024 there have been advances in many of the areas covered in that edition. As such, we updated the book in this second edition to reflect the latest developments in artificial intelligence, including recent breakthroughs in multimodal AI systems, advances in AI safety research, and emerging applications across various industries. Just remember, AI moves at an incredible tempo and we will recommend different ways to stay as up to date as possible.

However, we still focus on the **principles**, **processes** and **underpinnings** that make up artificial intelligence, these concepts remain and understanding them will go a long way to improving your understanding of this field.

This is **not** intended as a deeply technical book, but rather a window into what lies underneath the all-encompassing realm of artificial intelligence. Having a Guru to help us on our journey of discovery will no doubt help us!

David Bruce
Cambridge, England
2025

How to use this book

While this book is designed to be read sequentially, **each** chapter stands as a comprehensive unit you can explore based on your interests.

Whether you're curious about large language models like GPT-4, interested in how companies like OpenAI, Anthropic, Meta and Microsoft are shaping the future, or want to understand the latest developments in artificial intelligence, you can navigate directly to the specific chapter that can be read in isolation.

However, reading them sequentially is recommended as you will build your understanding in a logical manner, especially as we cover core concepts.

This is **not** a coursebook on AI, when technical concepts are necessary, we will break them down into clear, easily digestible explanations.

Our focus is on **clarity** and **understanding**. Each chapter concludes with a glossary of key terms and concepts to reinforce your understanding.

The book is structured into these core sections:

- **Introduction: First things first**
  An overview of AI's current state and its rapid evolution in recent years
- **Foundations of AI: The building blocks**
  From basic algorithms to advanced neural networks and transformer architectures
- **Key Technologies: What the heck is a large language model? What's a Transformer?**

Deep dives into large language models, computer vision, and other cornerstone AI technologies

- **Industry Leaders: The Big Players**
  Analysis of major AI companies, research labs, and their contributions to the field
- **Hardware and Infrastructure: I need Iron, lots of Iron...**
  Understanding the computational backbone of AI systems, including specialized processors and quantum computing developments
- **Ethics and Safety: Keeping us safe**
  Critical examination of AI alignment, safety measures, and ethical considerations
- **Future Trajectories: Visions of an AI Future, the end of work?**
  Exploring potential paths for AI development and their societal implications
- **Practical Applications: Getting Started with AI**
  Hands-on guidance for working with AI tools and understanding their real-world applications

Like every journey, we need to start with a single step, so let's look at how this all started...

Introduction

AI: The Future Is Overdue*[1]

Artificial intelligence is everywhere. Frenzied media reports of AI making millions unemployed, destroying entire industries and fundamentally altering our lives occur every day. But what exactly is it, how does it work and how will it actually impact our lives?

This book aims to provide a map that will not only provide a solid foundation but also drive you to explore further, exploring AI apps and tools, experimenting with them and taking advantage of what they have to offer.

The parallels with other transformative technologies are there. The rise of the automobile doing away with the horse. The PC destroying the concept of the telephone operator and the typist, the cell phone obliterating many industries and upending others such as the music industry.

However, the difference with AI is the **pace** of change and **rates** of adoption. Rates of adoption of AI are on a scale not seen before. When ChatGPT was first made available in November 2022, it was like the whole world discovered it overnight. Within two months, a hundred million people were using it—that's faster than TikTok, Instagram, or pretty much anything else we've seen. And that was just the beginning.

Since then, we've seen even more impressive AI systems like GPT-4, Claude, and Gemini pop up, each doing things that seemed impossible just months before.

---

[1] With thanks to the group ***Nothing but Thieves,*** strongly recommended.

Within the first week more than **one million** had signed up to access it. In two months more than one hundred million were using AI.

Up until the release of ChatGPT by the OpenAI corporation the use of AI was seen as more niche in large part due to the less user-friendly ways of directly accessing it.

This is **not** to say that many of us weren't already using AI without realising it. Examples such as Netflix recommendations, using Apple's Siri or Google Maps to navigate the most efficient route all incorporate machine learning algorithms that are a fundamental part of artificial intelligence.

However, with the advent of ChatGPT the sheer scale of the jump in capability was remarkable. Instead of just asking Google "*What's the weather like in Berlin*?" you can have an AI help you plan an entire trip to Germany, complete with custom itineraries based on your interests, budget, and travel style.

Want to write a song? AI can help with that. Need to design a logo? It can do that too. Have an idea for an entire movie? AI can do that as well..

On the surface this is pure originality; the system is making up a text of great depth and shows real creativity. Yet the reality is more complex than this and one we will explore in more detail in this book.

Think of it more like the world's most sophisticated *pattern-matching system*. It's been trained on massive amounts of data and can combine and remix that information in incredibly clever ways, but it's not actually conscious or creative in the way humans are, yet, and yes we will discuss future implications of sentience.

At its core then AI is the attempt to make machines (computers) think *like* humans. To show intelligence by taking information that we already know, combine it with logical reasoning and come up with an 'intelligent' answer.

1: First things first

'The future is here; it's just unevenly distributed.' – William Gibson

How did we get here?

A common misconception is that AI sort of 'appeared' out of nowhere in the last few years. In reality there are academic papers dating back to the early 1900s discussing *intelligent machines*.

World War II proved to be a crucial catalyst in computing history. The urgent need to decrypt enemy communications—most famously the Enigma machine's codes—led to the development of the first true computers.

These machines, designed to process millions of possible cipher (code) combinations, laid the groundwork for modern computing. Among the brilliant minds working on this project was Alan Turing, who saw far beyond the immediate military applications.

Turing proposed something revolutionary: a machine that could demonstrate intelligence by convincingly imitating human behaviour.

This idea evolved into the famous "**Turing Test**," where a machine would attempt to engage in conversation so naturally that humans couldn't distinguish it from a real person. While computing power at the time made this impossible to achieve, the concept helped shape our understanding of artificial intelligence.

However, restrictions on computing power meant that all of this was purely theoretical, they simply didn't have the "horsepower" to operate at that level.[2]

However, the first appearance of the term *artificial intelligence* was in the 1950s as the first digital computers came on the scene. These were incredibly rudimentary machines compared to what we are used to now but they were a big jump in capability compared to their Second World War forerunners.

Key individuals such as John McCarthy formed what was called the *Dartmouth Movement*. This brought together experts in mathematics, computer science (a very new discipline at that time) as well as languages and psychology. Together they worked on the fundamentals of how systems could reason, problem solve and even think, in essence, **Artificial Intelligence** as McCarthy called it.

The real transformation began in the early 2000s, when computing power finally caught up with these theoretical ambitions. Progress followed a clear progression:[3]

- **Handwriting recognition**
- **Speech recognition**
- **Image processing**
- **Natural language understanding**
- **Advanced language generation**

Several key organizations drove this evolution:

---

2 *When discussing computer "horsepower," we're referring to processing capability—specifically, the number of calculations a system can execute simultaneously. This is determined by factors such as memory capacity and CPU (Central Processing Unit) specifications, which together enable many tasks to be completed by a computer in parallel*

3 *we will explore this in later chapters when we talk about multi-modal capabilities.*

- **Nvidia** pioneered specialized hardware and software for AI applications
- **Google** invested heavily in large language models and neural networks
- **OpenAI** revolutionized public perception with ChatGPT

Before exploring these developments in detail, it's essential to understand the fundamental concepts that power modern AI. Throughout this book, we'll examine:

- **Large language models**
- **Neural networks**
- **Machine learning**
- **Training data**
- **Autonomous systems**

Each of these components plays a crucial role in the AI systems we interact with today, from virtual assistants to autonomous vehicles.

Key things:

- Concepts of AI are not new and date back at least to the early 1900s, and conceptual papers were written even before that time.

- The Dartmouth Movement in the 1950s kick-started the process of investigating what technologies and models would be needed to build AI systems.

- A blend of computer science, logic, algorithms and computing power were all identified as needed for working AI models.

2: Different Layers of AI

So, in order to create an AI system, you need three things:

- **Training data**: the more the better. Think of all the available information that is readily available online as well as books, documents and more. Specifically:

    - Digital content from across the internet
    - Digitized books and academic papers
    - Structured databases
    - Documentation across various fields
    - Real-world data from sensors and devices

- **Algorithms**: a series of *rules* or *instructions* that tell the system what it is expected to do. They power what are called LLMs (large language models).

- **Computing power**: the more you can harness the better, specifically the computational resources needed to process and analyse **vast** amounts of data.

The first two we have had in relative abundance over many years.

However, computing power has lagged behind what we have wanted to do in AI until relatively recently but two key developments have changed this landscape, namely the emergence of **cloud computing infrastructure** and substantial investments from technology companies that possess both:

- **Massive data centres**
- **Cash, lots of cash…**

But first, there are many ways of grouping AI capabilities. Most centre around moving from the **simplest** to the most **complex**. Bear in mind that the most complex ones are still as of time of writing theoretical but given the rate of change in AI likely to manifest sooner rather than later. Have a look at the diagram, start at the bottom, from simplest to the top, most complex.

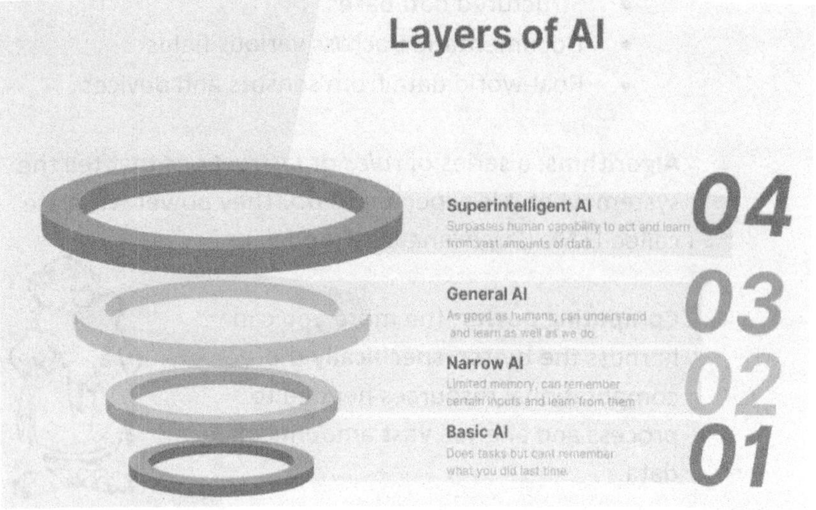

Artificial intelligence systems exist on a progressive spectrum of capability, with each tier building upon the foundations of previous levels. Currently, only the first two tiers—Basic AI and Narrow AI—have been realised, while AGI (Artificial General Intelligence) and Superintelligent AI remain theoretical concepts.[4]

---

[4] As far as is publicly known, rumours of General AI systems that are actually in existence are rife in the AI community but proving these rumours is more challenging.

The first, **Basic AI** is, as the term suggests, a form of AI that works in a simplistic form focused on a specific set of rules. Examples of basic AI include smart thermostats that respond to different temperatures or an AI opponent in a game such as chess.

These systems follow predefined paths and have no memory as such. By memory, we mean that at this level, the computer systems won't recognise a move that you may have played yesterday or that another player has used to win a game.

Basic AI:

- **Rule-based decision making**
- **Single-task focus**
- **Can't remember**
- **Predetermined response patterns**

Moving to the next level we have what is called **Narrow** (sometimes called **low memory) AI**. This **does** store the information from what has occurred previously and is data-driven. Examples of this include Siri from Apple or Alexa from Amazon. These systems use machine learning, a concept we will look at in depth in later chapters, to respond to your requests with the 'best fit' answers.

However, the answers it can give are limited, it cannot show judgement and it attempts to imitate opinions if asked specific questions. Siri or Alexa do not actually have opinions; the responses have been programmed by its developers. You will recognise this if you have chatted with a chatbot and it gets confused very easily!

Narrow differs from Basic AI due to its greater capabilities. These are enabled by the four elements below. We will cover these concepts in later chapters, for now just know that Narrow AI is more powerful and capable than Basic AI.

- **Machine learning implementation**
- **Data retention and historical context**
- **Pattern recognition**
- **Contextual response generation**

One of the best-known narrow AI systems is ChatGPT (GPT stands for chat **Generative Pre-trained Transformer**). This large language model, developed by the OpenAI Corporation, attempts to give detailed and highly constructive responses to inputs typed in by the user. Despite the sophistication of ChatGPT it is still (as of time of writing) narrow AI.

It cannot recognise images without specific guidance or play an online poker game for example. However, huge amounts of work are being done on what is called multimodal LLMs. These **can** recognise text, sounds, video, code and combine them to create a valid response. For example, recognise a drawing of a house, make a song and a story about this and then create a sixty-second video.

The core of ChatGPT (and other AI systems) is a large language model trained on huge amounts of data available in the public domain. This is then refined using feedback from humans; for example, was the answer that was generated correct or did it need improvement? In addition, it uses neural networks, a system that uses multiple levels to improve the quality of data returned.

This approach is not confined to ChatGPT, other advanced prompt systems such as Grok from X , Bard from Google also use these principles as well as huge amounts of processing power.

They are improving at an incredible rate but they are still focused on specific tasks, giving me a very clear response to what I have typed in, using specific styles and at the level of detail that I require. They are incredibly sophisticated but are not infallible.

Specifically, the answers given are not always correct and there are times when these systems create what are called '*hallucinations*'. This is where AI actually makes up answers to prompts and is a cause for a lot of concern amongst tech companies. We will explore this area in much more detail in Chapter 21.

Key things:

- You need training data, algorithms (large language models) and computing power for AI to work.
- There are four levels of AI: basic, narrow, general and superintelligent. The first two exist already.
- Basic can manage predetermined response patterns but it can't remember the thread of what it has been asked previously.
- Narrow can remember and starts to really use machine learning which we will discuss in depth in chapter 8.
- AGI (General) and Superintelligent AI don't exist yet, however rumours abound of tech companies making breakthroughs in these areas.

3: The Next Layer

'The idea is that the machine should be like a human being, and imitate the human being in detail.' – Alan Turing

So, we have our first two systems, basic and narrow. These exist and are being developed and improved all the time. The next two are, for now, theoretical and lie at the heart of what we consider true artificial intelligence, at least as formulated in countless science fiction books and movies.

General AI, often named AGI, is a category of AI that has many more abilities than the narrow, tightly focused levels we have just described in Chapter 2. This is AI that can learn, reason and, to an extent comparable to a human, actually apply what has been 'learned'. As a result, AGI is to all intents and purposes humanlike in intelligence. It can reason, adapt its outputs based on varying inputs and output just as a human would. Remember though, it's still theoretical.

Just as humans take in information through their senses, a true AGI system is **multimodal**, meaning that it can learn from speech, images, code and text and create a reasoned response. We already have multimodal elements as part of narrow AI; for example, there are healthcare AI systems that combine inputs from scans (images) with patient records (text) and create an almost instant diagnostic profile for the physician.

However, these are by their nature narrow in breadth (in the example, focused on the healthcare domain) and straying outside the strict boundaries of this leads to unclear responses. But the potential is there. Let's explore what could be possible with an AGI healthcare solution:

A doctor's surgery in the near future

Your doctor welcomes you into her diagnostic room. She advises you that she will be using **AI Medi** (a hypothetical AI assistant) to assist her.

You explain your symptoms; she takes specific readings such as blood pressure and asks her (human) assistant to conduct a chest X-ray. While all of this is happening, the AI Medi is doing the following:

- Analysing and transcribing all of the conversation between you and the doctor, gaining and extracting insights from the dialogue (speech) including stressors.

- Instantly analysing all historical health-related data that is on your file and looking for patterns, trends and possible causalities related to the current condition (text) and comparing to millions of data sets.

- Reviewing not only the images from the current X-ray but instantly comparing this to previous X-rays and looking for any changes, comparing the images to hundreds of thousands of X-rays from similar demographics (imaging).

Then in the final ten minutes of the consultation the AGI produces a diagnosis, suggests a course or possible courses of action, potentially surgical intervention or medication.

All of this is highly tailored to **you specifically**, taking into account the most successful treatments that have already been used worldwide. This does not take the doctor out of the equation; instead, it empowers the doctor to assess the AI Medi outputs, and where **specific choices** are offered, select what they consider the most appropriate.

Currently, for doctors, a key element of what takes a large amount of their time is transcribing patient notes from the consultation, noting the course of treatment as planned, including medication dosages and possibly writing prescriptions.

We do have something that takes us part of the way there already, **Google AMIE**, the Articulated Medical Intelligence Explorer. It may have a clunky name but it is a potentially incredibly useful medical diagnostic tool.

It works as an online text-based medical consultation system by interacting with a patient, just as a physician would do, asking specific questions via a chat prompt.

Initial testing of this through double-blind approaches, that is, the patient doesn't know whether they are dealing with a doctor or an AI system, has been very positive, especially with rarer illnesses and more unusual symptoms.

Remember though, AMIE is **not** an AGI system, it's an advanced narrow AI system focused on medical diagnostics. Stray outside of those boundaries and it gets stumped very quickly.

AGI systems will potentially do all of this in real time in the future; the doctor can then review and approve or make changes as needed. This lets the doctor focus on what they are really good at, assessing and providing healthcare, with the drudgery removed from the process.

The information provided by the AI Medi is also constantly being updated with new drug and medical discoveries, just as all large language models get updated as new data emerges. As these new data, treatments and medical interventions emerge, via medical journals, scientific research and other forms of published data, the AI model will adjust and incorporate these findings into possible treatment plans.

So, AGI is the next level up from where we are now, but there is another level, one that surpasses what humans can do and it's called superintelligence....

Key things:

- AGI or artificial general intelligence looks to mimic the capabilities of a human. It isn't confined to one specific task, like being an expert in chess; rather it is the ability to do multitude of tasks.
- AGI doesn't exist yet although a number of AI corporations claim they are close.

4: Superintelligence

'We can remember it for you wholesale.' – Philip K Dick

While AGI remains in the future, ASI, or artificial superintelligence, is even further away. While AGI is designed to emulate human capabilities, ASI is designed to exceed human capabilities in **multiple** domains.

Again, the key here is multiple domains. For instance, AI systems like IBM's Deep Blue and Google DeepMind's AlphaGo have already surpassed us in **specific** areas such as chess or Go, games that are massively complex yet still have very clear, agreed-upon rules.

AI superintelligence takes this many stages further, surpassing our capabilities in multiple domains, while researching, formulating and testing new concepts and theories. All using what are called recursive or learning models to improve upon and advance what is already known.

An ASI would also potentially be self-aware, something that has preoccupied AI researchers for many years (not to mention science fiction authors). ASI could in theory understand and interpret human emotions and respond accordingly.

Some of the potential applications for an ASI include:

Medical research: Proposing and testing entirely new drug combinations for medical treatments, using all the world's available data on drugs. The work on an mRNA vaccine for Covid-19 relied upon narrow AI to sequence millions of possible combinations and shortlist them for human trials. An ASI system would go further, simulating human trials as well as possible combinations and massively accelerating advances in medicine.

Space exploration: Travelling to planets and moons in the solar system, conducting research and paving the way for human exploration, all conducted autonomously.

Financial analysis: Analysing market data from all the world's stock markets, identifying trends and executing trades, all in nanoseconds and all autonomously. Current large financial firms **have** already built their own proprietary trading systems that learn from past events but these are rangebound and their freedom to trade is limited by strict parameters.

Robot assistants that are ASI enabled. These build a complete understanding of the human that they are assisting, they can read their moods, care for them and provide completely unique/customised care.

These are all *theoretical* applications of ASI, the possible applications of ASI are likely infinite. However, with this huge potential comes concerns. With a system that is *potentially* self-aware, how can we define what rights it has? Should it pay tax if it replaces the job of a human who certainly would have to? What ethical rules should be in place to govern how ASI is used?

Such questions have been asked for years by researchers in AI and principles of use for ASI have been put forward. There are still large divergences in how different organisations approach these issues and they will become more important as AI and guardrails around ASI develop.

However, we aren't at ASI yet. There are some major advances still needed to make this a reality. These include:

- Even more powerful computing capabilities, possibly even quantum computing.

- Highly advanced language learning models (LLMs).
- The ability to use existing data to extrapolate and apply to unseen or unknown situations.
- Multimodal (text, video, natural language, code) comprehensions and application to new domains.

None of these are trivial breakthroughs; however, we have recently seen huge breakthroughs and improvements in all of these areas, most notably the multimodal[5] capabilities of AI. We will dig deeper into these in turn as they form the core of AI systems both real and theoretical.

Key things:

- Superintelligence is a form of AI that completes a multitude of tasks better than a human. Each task, for example financial analysis, is performed at a far superior level to a human professional.

- It doesn't exist yet but it does exist in **a lot** of movies, check out the character of David in the Ridley Scott movie *Prometheus* for an example.

- Don't discount the use of movies in foretelling possible futures that incorporate superintelligence in robotic forms, **iRobot** and **Bladerunner** showing where we may be headed.

[5] Multimodal being the ability to create text, images, video, sound and more using AI.

5: Key Concepts – Generative AI

Generative AI, or the products linked with AI, is core to what most people think of when the term AI is raised. It refers to AI that generates nominally 'new' work; for example, when you ask ChatGPT to write you a story about the Roman empire in five hundred words, it creates this original new text for you. Likewise, if you ask Dall-E to create an image of dogs playing cards in the style of Renoir, an original image is created.

Modern generative AI relies on advanced neural network architectures, primarily transformer models and large language models (LLMs), which differ significantly from the original Generative Adversarial Network (GAN) concept. While Ian Goodfellow's GAN was an important milestone in AI development, current generative AI uses more complex approaches.

For text generation, models like GPT (Generative Pre-trained Transformer) use:

- Massive training datasets: **data, lots of data..**
- Sophisticated neural network architectures: **like a brain made of computer connections that gets smarter by practicing, just like you learn by playing a game over and over.**

- Probabilistic prediction of likely word sequences: **what word is likely to come next after the word "rainy"?**
- Contextual understanding through attention mechanisms: **Is this text about life in ancient Rome? If**

so that context needs to be taken into account but context understanding is limited.

It's not quite Human....it has some limitations:

- All outputs are based strictly on training data, you need good quality training data
- No genuine comprehension or independent reasoning, it can't reason for you...
- Potential for generating biased or incorrect information
- Lack of true creativity or original thought, it's not Picasso no matter how much you want it to be..

Imagine a powerful AI model, similar to the type used in large language models, trying to replicate the artistic style of Claude Monet. Instead of writing text, the model is trained on a collection of hundreds of Monet's paintings, learning patterns like his use of colours, brushstrokes, and the way he composed his scenes.[6]

The AI doesn't copy any specific Monet painting directly. Rather it creates something new by predicting what a Monet-style painting **should look like** based on the patterns it has learned. This is similar to how language models predict the next word in a sentence, except here the AI predicts how different parts of an image should look and fit together.

If the model produces an image that doesn't quite match Monet's style—maybe the colours don't feel right, or the brushstrokes look off—it adjusts itself and tries again. This process repeats, with the model improving its output step by

[6] It helps that Monet painted over 2000 paintings in his lifetime. Think of this as the "training data" for the AI model.

step until it creates an image that closely resembles something Monet might have painted.

This idea works not just for images but also for text and even code. The model keeps refining its results based on feedback from the patterns it has learned. However, it's important to understand that the AI doesn't truly "understand" Monet's art or his intentions. It's simply imitating what it has been trained to recognize as "Monet-like."

The quality of what the AI creates depends on the quality of the training data. If the data isn't very good—like low-quality images or incomplete examples—the AI's results will reflect those flaws. But with enough good data and practice, the model can produce impressive, almost lifelike imitations of Monet's style, based on the patterns it has been taught.

Remember: Data+ Patterns+Iterations: you get an approximation of what a Monet painting original might look like.

Key things:

- AI models in the past used GAN, a system that permitted generative AI to work using an adversarial approach to text and image generation.

- Modern AI systems now use a blend of transformer models and large language models to create text, images or sound.

  (*Don't worry, we will discuss transformer models in Chapter 7. For the moment just remember we need them in order to make generative AI work*)

- Generative AI does **not** work like a human brain does to generate novel work due to the following things it needs to do:

  - Analyse statistical patterns in training data
  - Predict probable next tokens (words or image pixels)
  - It does not truly "understand" content in a human sense
  - Rely entirely on sophisticated pattern recognition

6: Key Concepts – Large Language Models

'Nobody phrases it this way, but I think that artificial intelligence is almost a humanities discipline. It's really an attempt to understand human intelligence and human cognition.'

– Sebastian Thrun

What is a large language model (**LLM**)?

LLMs attempt to mimic how we as humans communicate, the patterns, structures and flows of languages, something called natural language processing, in order to create new text, images, sounds and more.

It's a large computer model that is **general** in purpose and can be pre-trained and then fine-tuned as needed for **specific areas**, domains or applications.

The big guns in this space are:

OpenAI:	GPT-4 (and higher as they release so frequently)
Meta:	Falcon
X:	Grok
Apple:	Llama
Microsoft:	AutoGen
Google:	PaLM 2

As well as major innovators such as Amazon and Tesla.

LLMs are not restricted to English; they cater for more than one hundred different languages. However, the training data (the supply of books and other training material) reduces the more obscure the language becomes and hence the outputs in those languages will be less accurate. LLMs rely on what is called a **transformer**, which is key to them working effectively.

So, when we type into ChatGPT—for example, *Write me a story about eighteenth-century London in the style of Charles Dickens*—the LLM, which as part of its training has been trained on all the works of Dickens, can create a story in the style requested almost instantly as it has learned the patterns, connections and structures in the data contained in existing Dickens's books.

There are three elements at play here:

1) The enormous training **data set**, often counted in petabytes.[7] The training data ingested by LLMs has become a source of controversy as authors and publications object to their copyrighted text being used to train models. A number of companies involved in AI now give the creator the option of having their work omitted from training to address this issue.

2) The **parameters**, which are the elements that the model uses and adjusts during training. They are key to how the transformer model works in that they form part of the process to make predictions. Similar to adjusting the settings in a car to get the perfect temperature.

3) The **transformer model**: This is the heart (or brain?) of an LLM, and is a form of neural network that is able to take in commands and output content by using what are called attention mechanisms, the way in which it understands the linkages and meanings between words. We will explore transformers further in the next chapter.

---

[7] A petabyte is the same as 500 billion pages of standard text.

The LLM has a predicted value and an actual value in the training data. The closer the predicted value, for example **Grass is Green**, matches the training data where **Grass is Green** occurs multiple times, the better.[8]

For example, one aim of LLMs is to predict the next word in a sentence through exposure to huge data sets and training on the occurrence of words in a logical manner. For instance, ***The sea is ...*** may initially return a random word such as **rabbit**. However, as it is trained, it will encounter such phrases that it will begin to return responses such as ***The sea is blue, The sea is cold*** and so on.

If we type into one of the large language models such as ChatGPT or Grok— *Tell me ten facts about sheepdogs*—the LLM will generate a response based on the huge amounts of data already learned and trained upon through ingestion and parametrisation of the data.

Each iteration or update of the LLM should be improved through feedback by the end or internal users, which is why a lot of models ask you to rate the accuracy of the response you received. Persistently incorrect responses should in time be corrected.

LLMs can be used for many different tasks that we need to solve, not just text manipulation but also image generation, language translation and more. Even better, fine-tuning them does not need anything like the same size data as for the initial pre-training, so small data sets are sufficient to give effective responses.

[8] Google's PaLM 2 has more than 500 billion parameters.

However, they are **not** infallible, they can make mistakes if the original training data is incorrect, out of date or simply does not exist. There are other factors at play as well and we cover this more in Chapter 20 where we look at mistakes that can be made by LLMs called **hallucinations**. [9]

That is at the general level but what if we want something tailored, maybe specific to the business I work in or profession? LLMs can help with this too. Imagine we work in a law firm and need tens of thousands of documents parsed very quickly without omitting key legal data. The LLM is used in the following way:

1) **Pre-trained**: The large language model is exposed to legal documentation that the firms possesses, for example in the legal claims area.

2) **Fine-tuned**: The model is then fine-tuned by looking at success or failure of legal claims over the last ten years, pulling out key elements that resulted in success (or failure) of claims.

Then, exposing future claims to this LLM gives the law firm's employees a ranking of their possible success probability and helping their decision process whether to pursue a claim or not.

Remember, LLM's are built around prediction and probabilities.

[9] A fancy name for AI making answers up. We will talk a lot about this in detail in Chapter 21 *"**Do Androids Dream of Electric Sheep?**"*

Key things:

- LLMS are the core of AI systems.
- Trained on huge data sets, uses a transformer (that converts data into numbers) in order to understand specific patterns.
- Relies on prediction to create the next word in a sentence.
- Can be fine-tuned for specific industries, such as law, finance or marketing.
- While LLM's are powerful they do have inherent limitations in reasoning and factual accuracy, they **aren't** infallible.

7: Key Concepts – Transformers: Robots in Disguise

More than meet the eye ...

The name ChatGPT stands for **chat generative pre-trained transformer**. We need to look at the transformer bit and explain it in more detail. We have already looked at the importance of good training data for AI systems to work accurately, so the next step is for the AI system to learn from that data and predict the next word (if it is text-based, just as ChatGPT is).

Natural language processing is the process by which AI models understand and respond to questions posed in what we call natural or normal language. Now in order for an AI system to perform natural language processing it needs to use what is called a transformer model. Unfortunately, it's not like the cool robots from the 1980s that turned into cars and planes, rather it is a clever way of getting the model to pay more or less attention to **specific** words in a sentence.[10]

Let's use an example such as we are learning French and we want to ask someone what the weather is going to be like today. So, we have our input, which will be in English:

The input: 'Good morning, will it rain today?'
The transformer takes this input and goes through a number of steps, converting each word into a series of numbers (vectors) and then processing each part of the sentence in order to try and understand not only the words themselves but their context. So, in this case the transformer model should recognise first that this is a question and then that the context is a

[10] This is quite a simplified example, there is **a lot** more happening under the hood but the principles hold.

question about the weather.

The output: Armed with the context and meaning of each word the transformer model then attempts to create the output, using what is called a self-attention approach, to generate each word of the response **'Bonjour, va-t-il pleuvoir aujourd-hui?'.** This is done using what is called a decoder.

So, some key concepts make up the transformer model, they are:

Context: What is being asked here? Is this a question? What is the context of that question? Sometimes referred to as the semantic meaning of the words. In reality, it means considering the meaning of the sentence as a whole, not viewing each word in isolation. However, some words are more important than others, so it needs to pay more attention to those.

Attention: This is where keywords in the sentence are assigned a higher weighting or importance. In our example above this would be the **rain** element. Note that there is usually more than one attention mechanism at work.

The wild success of OpenAI's ChatGPT is down in no small part to their sophisticated transformer models. These have been trained on huge data sets[11], in the order of between 500 billion to 1.5 trillion machine learning parameters so that even though the system may never have been asked the specific question you ask before, it can understand the context and weighting of your question enough to generate an answer that (usually) is what you are looking for.

[11] GPT4 has about 1.5trn parameters, Claude 3 Opus has slightly fewer at 1 trillion.

Key things:

- Transformers convert data into numbers, hence the name. This makes it much easier for the algorithms to recognise patterns.
- Transformers use attention-weighting algorithms to understand what keywords in a sentence are.
- They have a limited understanding of the context of a word and sentence. For example, is this a question or a statement?
- AI systems are easily confused by context, notably in some fields such as geometry; like everything in AI these contextual issues are being addressed.

8: Key Concepts – Machine Learning

'Science is organised knowledge.' – Herbert Spencer

Remember we need three elements for an AI system:

- **Data**
- **Algorithms (rules)**
- **Computing power**

All of these are integral to machine learning (ML), which is a subset of artificial intelligence itself. It is an attempt to use algorithms and computer models to execute tasks without needing to be **explicitly** programmed. The idea is to access data and learn **patterns** and **probabilities** from this and if correctly designed the model should improve over time. When people talk about artificial intelligence this is very frequently what they are referring to.

This doesn't sound very ground-breaking but if you look at how all current non-AI computer systems work, they have a set of **rules** and execute against them. They have to be told explicitly to do (or not do) something. Some older robot systems used in manufacturing will keep painting a panel of a vehicle even if that panel is not there, in essence painting thin air. Newer systems have very sophisticated sensors that stop this from happening; however, this is all still pre-programmed with clearly defined parameters.

Machine learning is different. It attempts to execute tasks without being explicitly told what to do. We don't give the ML specific instructions, instead the algorithm is designed to learn from the data and recognise patterns. Instead of being told exactly how to travel from A to B, we are providing a map, compass and a mode of transport, the system then needs to figure out the best route.

The healthcare example in Chapter 3, where the AI-enabled doctor was able to prescribe specific and highly targeted drugs for the patient with a very high level of accuracy, is an example of machine learning. The ML algorithm learns from the millions of data records for patients of the same age, medical conditions and the outcomes for these patients. This algorithm hasn't been specifically programmed to prescribe drugs for the specific patient, rather it is a general prescription engine.

As such, by identifying patterns of successful treatment for thousands of patients in the past with similar conditions—the drugs chosen, dosage cycles and so on—the machine learning system can then prescribe drugs with a high level of accuracy. There is more going on under the hood (for example iteration cycles) but the concepts stand and help us understand the power of ML in Medicine.[12]

Another example is traffic sign recognition used in autonomous vehicles. The ML system is not designed to know that it needs to stop at the specific stop sign at the end of your street. However, it is designed to recognise what a stop sign looks like and to react accordingly. For example, the ML system designed by Mercedes Benz in their newest vehicles learns your patterns of usage. In the winter time if you normally switch on the heated steering wheel after you switch on the heated seats the car will learn this pattern of behaviour and do it automatically for you.[13]

---

[12] We do need to be aware of ethical concerns related to medicine and machine learning, such as bias, privacy and date protection amongst others. These are not resolved and are likely to come to the fore as medicine embraces AI.

[13] Note that this is a simple form of personalisation Machine learning.

So, how does it work? At a high level, machine learning operates across four key stages:

- **Collect data**: Could be thousands of images of stop signs, millions of prescription drug records, buyer behaviours.
- **Recognise patterns in the data**: Most stop signs tend to be red with white lettering, they are generally a specific shape.
- **Learn from all the patterns**: That sign that my car sensing cameras have picked up is very likely to be a stop sign. This is an iterative process, i.e. it repeats
- **Make a decision**: I'd better stop.

Key things:

- Machine learning lets AI execute tasks without being explicitly told what to do step by step unlike most current computer systems.
- It uses the collect→ recognise→learn model.
- Machine learning relies on learning patterns in data.

9: Key Concepts – Deep Learning and Neural Networks

You are driving down the highway in your Tesla car. Your vehicle is using the **autopilot** feature, this enables the car to steer, brake and change direction by itself (as long as the driver is paying attention). On your left a car comes alongside you and moves slightly ahead, then it swerves into your lane. Your car immediately brakes and steers you to the right out of harm's way.

All of this happens in far less than a second. You may have been able to react in time if you were in control yourself, maybe not. Regardless, you avoided a potentially serious crash. This is one example of a neural network in action.

Tesla's autopilot and FSD systems are neural networks. They assesses images from all the cameras mounted outside the vehicle (inputs) using what is called Tesla RegNet. This analyses all the different elements or layers of images captured.

Crucially the car takes this input and uses it to decide what to do next, for example, should I slow down as there is a red light ahead? Or very usefully, swerve out of the way to avoid a car about to crash into me. This is different to radar, cruise control systems because the car maintains a constant bubble, called Vector Space Data, around the vehicle. For example, it won't swerve into another line if a truck is right beside me, it will brake instead. This is the output.

'Prediction is very difficult, especially about the future.' – Niels Bohr

We looked at machine learning in the previous chapter and if you think of machine learning as AI at its highest level, using algorithms that learn from data or examples, then deep learning is one of its **subfields**. Deep learning is called this as it uses neural networks that go deep, hence the name.

Neural networks are an attempt to mimic the workings of the human brain, or at least how we **think** the human brain works. The neural networks are made up of many layers, which are made up of **nodes**.[14]

The first layers are part of the input function while the last is, of course, the output layer. As a piece of data makes its way through each layer (and usually there are more than five) it is assigned a **weighting** for how important or not that piece of information is. The real power of this system is how complex and, well, deep it is. The more layers and parameters the more that can be learned from the data. This is super useful when you are dealing with what is called unstructured or random data.

The aim is to classify, interpret and make decisions based on data, be it code, images or text. The key part of a neural network is that it can **predict** what should happen next, in essence make a high-quality decision that forms the output. In between the input (the data) and the output (could be text, code, image or the movements of a robot/vehicle for example) are a series of computing layers, each one giving a weighting to the next level, just as seen with the Tesla example.

---

[14] A node is actually a mathematical function that mimics the workings of a biological neuron. It's a brilliant idea and pretty complex. The actual function is this: $f(w_1x_1 + w_2 x_2 + \dots + w_nx_n + b)$. Important to remember is the *w* represents weighting.

In reality there are many layers of neural networks at play here plus some very fancy algorithms (remember they are a set of rules to follow).

- **Tesla RegNet**: This takes in the images.
- **Tesla HydraNet**: Makes sense of the imagery.
- **Tesla Neural Net Planner**: Decides what to do; should it slow down, speed up, swerve?

All of this tries to replicate and improve upon how a human would drive. If the car had to send data back to a cloud computing system that could be an issue because of latency, or slowness. However, Tesla vehicles use what is called edge computing.[15] This is where the device, in this case the car, makes all the decisions itself in real time. The car simply doesn't have time to wait for a reply from a data centre, so instead the AI algorithms run in the car itself, allowing the car to react incredibly fast to risks and dangers.[16]

So, deep learning relies on neural networks. As data passes through each layer of the neural network, weightings are given to each element; the more layers that the data passes through, the higher the probability that accurate weightings will be applied. As a result, deep learning works really well with large amounts of **unstructured** data. The downside is that you need large amounts of computing power and of course data. This has held back the wider application of deep learning to systems such as self-driving cars or voice assistants until recently.

---

[15] See chapter 20 on edge computing for more details.

[16] There are entire YouTube channels devoted to Tesla vehicles getting their owners out of potential crashes. The system reaction times are quite something to watch.

Key things:

- Neural networks are an attempt to copy how a human brain works by predicting what the next action should be.
- They consist of **inputs** and **outputs**, governed by **weightings** that decide how important the inputs are and that influence what the outputs should be.
- Deep learning is incredibly powerful with unstructured big data.
- **Sparse neural networks** are all the rage now (2025) as they reduce the need for connections, in effect are far more efficient and thus reduce costs. It's a very cool idea made real, think of how our brains are incredibly adaptable following injury and how we heal around the damaged areas. This principle has been applied to sparse neural networks (and it works)

10: Key Concepts – Reinforcement Learning

'The only source of knowledge is experience.' – Albert Einstein

Reinforcement learning (RL) is one of the methods that machine learning uses to, well, learn and have the skills to do what we need it to do, for example, create realistic-sounding text in the style of the author James Joyce or recognise and categorise images.

It makes it more logical to look at what the goal of reinforcement learning is, which is to build what is called a **policy**, the strategy to be used in the algorithm. This policy could be used by Google to master the game of Go or by Meta to improve the realism of their Oculus VR headsets for example.

Just like we (usually) get better by playing a video game multiple times, when we learn what to do and what not to do in order to get higher scores, the same thing happens in reinforcement learning. It is described as reinforcement learning because we reward the **agent** (this is analogous to you playing a game) when it gets a task right and when it gets a task wrong it gets penalised.

States of mind

We let the agent loose in the training environment and we expose it to what are called **states**. A state is where we need the agent to make a decision, go left or go right? Dog or a cat? You could in theory let the agent loose and learn in the physical environment, for example control a vehicle, but that would be a *bit* risky.

We start reinforcement learning in virtual models, in this case this could be the layout of a standard city with the usual hazards. Every time the agent runs over a pedestrian, makes a dangerous move or breaks a speed limit it gets penalised. The opposite happens for good driving skills shown. The great thing about a simulated world is that you can easily throw random scenarios quickly at the agent, forcing it to make decisions that are rarer in real life and learn from them. Operating in low light levels, dealing with snowy conditions obscuring road markings, and tow trucks towing vehicles can all present challenging scenarios that need to be learned by the agent.

Eventually, the agent makes enough good decisions that the series of actions taken become codified, or baked, into the policy. This policy would then move to real-world testing, again with the agent making decisions and being either rewarded or penalised for actions taken (or not taken).

Reinforcement learning on games that have specific rules is especially powerful. When Google trained their RL algorithm called AlphaGo to master the game of Go it was so successful that the resulting policy (remember this is the sum of all its learning) was able to create entirely new moves and strategies that no one had used or thought of before. This revolutionised the way the game was played at the highest level, with top players adopting some of the tactics and stratagems the RL system had pioneered.

The impact on real world systems of RL occurs today. We have already looked at personalised healthcare examples (see chapter 3) and reinforcement algorithms (rules) are used to create highly tailored treatment plans for those undergoing chemotherapy or radiotherapy, an incredibly useful application. Other more mundane examples are supply chain optimisation. RL models build chains that are robust enough to manage disruptions (Chicago Ohare is snowbound, what other routes

can we use to get products to the stores on time?).
RL is also used in what are called multi-agent systems. Imagine a flying display of 100 drones. RL enables coordination as well as decentralised decision making (Basically making sure they create amazing designs in the sky while not bumping into each other).[17]

Key things:

- Reinforcement learning is like getting better at playing Pac-Man. You learn what works and what doesn't to improve the way you play.
- The **policy** is the result of all your learning, it means the next time you play the game you don't lose within a few seconds.
- Reinforcement learning relies on **agents** (you playing the game) and **states** (the game environment) to create the end **policy** (the best way to play and win).

[17] Military applications of this technology are obvious and worrying. Many nation states are working on refining and expanding on these capabilities.

The more training data that the system has the greater the level of certainty it has that what is displayed is correct. This forms part of what is called **supervised learning**. We present the system with one hundred different stop sign images and all of them are labelled as stop signs.

The next step is **semi-supervised learning**. We train the model by presenting it with one hundred more images, some of these will be labelled as stop signs, but the majority won't be and there will be some images that aren't stop signs at all.[19]

A different approach again is unsupervised **learning**. This uses unlabelled data and again the model must identify the stop signs in the set of images. It involves finding patterns in totally unlabelled data and uses techniques such as clustering or the excellently named dimensionality reduction.

The next step is that the machine learning algorithm (or system of rules) then takes the training data and can infer or predict what the next step is. This is called the **inference process.**

The maxim with training data is that to get a working model you need to go for quality over quantity. Garbage in, garbage out. So spending time on data cleansing is very important, removing unnecessary, poor-quality data means your model is more likely to work as intended. For supervised learning there is a lot more work required as you need to have **every** single data point labelled, image, text or code.

---

[19] We use semi-supervised data when labelling large datasets is just too expensive or not possible.

Key things:

- Training data follows the gather→clean→extract→train→check→tune approach.
- Three types of training data:
  - Supervised (tell it exactly how to handle every element)
  - Semi-supervised (tell it exactly how to handle some elements)
  - Unsupervised (figure it out yourself)

12: Key Concepts Training Data II – It's Mine, All Mine!

It's my data and I'll cry if I want to ...[20]

LLMs need a ton of data to train on. The more data that they are exposed to the better outputs for you the user. But what if they use your own data to train on? What does that mean for copyright, artistic control and of course revenue for authors and publications?

If you have ever published a blog or posted anything on a social media site it is possible that you have contributed to the data used to train one or several LLMs. When you interact with the LLM by typing prompts these are also used to train the models and is one of the reasons why LLMs always ask for feedback as this improves the model.

Each LLM, such as Google Gemini or Microsoft Copilot, will have different approaches to how they train their models but all of them have one thing in common: they need tons of data.

This data harvesting has raised major concerns about privacy and how this data is stored. We are seeing much more pushback from publications stating specifically that their output cannot be used for training purposes as well as artists stating their works cannot be used by users requesting an image 'in the style of artist X or Y'.

---

[20] With apologies to the singer Lesley Gore

We are likely to see developments in training data in the near future that will include the following:

– Compensation to authors/publications for the use of specific works in training data.

– Expansion of the ability to opt out of the use of your data for training purposes. It is possible at the moment by inserting tags on your website or blog but these can be ignored. Expect the rules around this to tighten up.

– Much stricter rules around data retention and usage, led by the EU. The EU has a bill coming forward called the EU AI Act, which looks to put guardrails around the use of training data. This bill will echo some of the legislation in GDPR, which describes data handling rules.

– Banning the use of any language model where the data is used by the LLM company. For example, more companies are now banning their staff from using ChatGPT entirely as the likelihood of sharing sensitive information is too great, what they really need are ...

– The creation of virtual private language models. Large companies with data sets will use off-the-shelf language models but will train them on their own data and the resulting model will only be accessible to company staff. Imagine IBM, Airbus or McDonald's being able to leverage all their existing data for new insights.

In summary, if you don't want your data used by LLMs then don't put it on the internet. If you want to make sure that your prompts aren't used by LLMs for training then you will need to use the business versions of OpenAI or Copilot. They offer by default the option of not storing and training from your prompts. This is understandable given the nature of what they offer to businesses that are reluctant to share any commercially sensitive information. Microsoft call this commercial data protection.

You can specify that you don't want your information stored and used for training purposes in ChatGPT consumer versions by adjusting the settings, which look something like this:

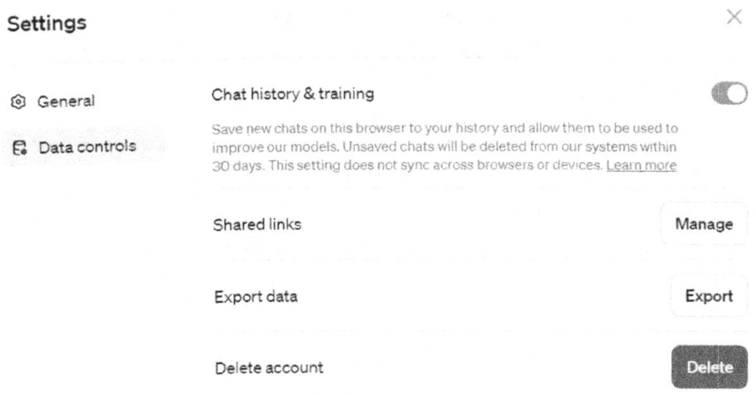

13: The Big Players in AI – Microsoft

[21]*Bring back Clippy!*

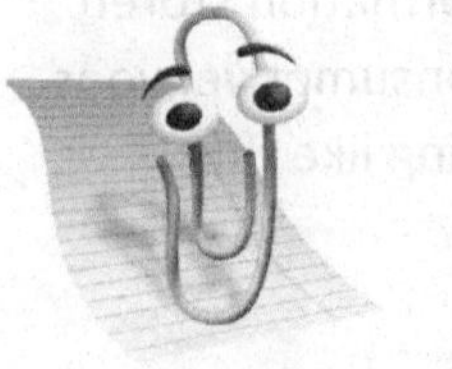

For those of you of a certain vintage, Clippy was the forerunner of Microsoft Copilot for Office 365 (O365). You would start typing in your Word document and it would pop up, with a little dialogue box saying, *'Hi, I see you're writing a document about widgets, would you like some help*?'

Then it would attempt to help with often hilarious results that generally were in no way connected to what you actually wanted to do. It wasn't a bad idea at all, it was just that the capability to be useful simply was somewhat lacking.

Microsoft (which also formed a strategic partnership with OpenAI as well and invested $10 billion) released its own product, part of the Bing browser, called Copilot. However, Copilot actually uses OpenAI technologies to produce results, so despite the branding, it is ultimately an OpenAI product under the hood. Similar to ChatGPT, this was a prompt system. This product led to much greater interest in Bing, which up until then had languished in the browser wars. With Copilot. Microsoft gave the option of three levels of responses, which other AI offerings did not have:

- **More creative**
- **More balanced**
- **More detailed**

---

[21] Clippy image © Microsoft Corporation.

The cost of building large language models, including training data, processing power and parameter tuning, means that development of AI systems has largely been the preserve of the likes of Google, Meta (Facebook) and Microsoft. We say largely as there have been some smaller companies that have made massive advances, most notably OpenAI.

OpenAI's technology stack for AI was not greatly different from the other big technology players; how it differed and really moved AI to the forefront was that they were the first company to put an interface forward for users linked to a robust LLM that was incredibly straightforward to use: simply type in a question or a request and your response is returned very quickly.

With its Copilot AI branding it is clear that Microsoft intends to integrate AI as much as possible into its ubiquitous Office suite, where working with Word, Excel and PowerPoint, the possibilities of AI creating, analysing and increasing the rate of output are readily apparent.

With Copilot for 0365 you have the ability to take the data that organisations create using their Office 365 tools and then apply AI to create the perfect PowerPoint presentation, summarise your company results in Excel or craft perfect sales copy in Word. This, in theory, is an incredibly powerful capability and Microsoft is going all in on this vision. Concerns about leaking sensitive information and data means that Microsoft doesn't share or use company information for model training purposes, which makes it much more popular and likely to be adopted by corporations that are very sensitive about what happens to their data. Their built-in safeguards around data encryption and data governance all aid in this approach for large corporations.

Key things:

- Microsoft aims to integrate AI into their key products such as Bing and O365.
- They actually use OpenAI under the hood for their products.
- They have a strategic relationship with OpenAI.
- Clippy is cool despite what everyone else says.
- Weirdly Clippy as a name in not recognised in the latest version of Microsoft Word, it's almost like they want to forget him (or her).

14: The Big Players in AI – OpenAI

First among equals

ChatGPT, when it was first unveiled in November 2022, made the news immediately. Until then, the concept of artificial intelligence, AI, had been an abstract concept for most individuals not working within the realms of computing research. With its arrival, incredibly rapid uptake (over one million within the first week) and the capabilities that even the first version showed suddenly had people asking about where it had come from and what was next to be developed.

The OpenAI corporation was started by a number of key individuals in 2015 who already had well-established positions of leadership in the technology space, most notably Elon Musk, but the current leader of OpenAI, Sam Altman, has gained enormous recognition since the introduction of ChatGPT as the face of OpenAI.

At its heart it had the goal of developing AGI technology with the mission of '*benefiting all humanity*'. Quite the aim. As we have discussed before, AGI is an AI system designed to replicate human behaviour in multiple domains rather than the narrow, more focused AI that we currently have available.

While **ChatGPT** is the best known of the products that OpenAI create they are also involved in many other areas that either benefit from AI, such as robotics, or directly using computer vision systems to develop autonomous vehicles.

In addition, their image generation model, **DALL-E**, is one of the most advanced AI solutions capable of creating realistic images and art from a natural language description.

They also have **Whisper**, a speech recognition model, which is able to transcribe, identify and translate across many different languages.

OpenAI also has a multitude of tools that support software developers building AI applications, for example, building a specific chatbot for a specific client. This is very powerful as it enables developers to fine-tune their answers by exposing the ChatGPT API[22] to their own company-specific data.

The AI systems that Open AI have developed rely on specific technologies, married together:

- **Large language models**
- **Deep learning/neural networks**
- **Transformer based models for its language models**
- **Very large data sets**
- **Natural language processing**

Their approach has been described as a two-step process; the first is to conduct a form of pre-training that evaluates how well the LLM predicts the next word in a sentence. This is done using data sets gleaned from the internet. The second part is the refinement stage, with humans in the loop, with the goal of improving the accuracy of the system and attempting to make responses more 'humanlike'.

Their use of very large data sets to train their models has been criticised as the source of this information has been as much of

---

[22] API: Application programming interface – think of it as a pipeline linking different parts of a program together.

the world's information that is readily accessible. Newspapers and authors have expressed concern at their own works being used to train OpenAI's models without any form of compensation. In responding to this OpenAI has made policy changes and attempted to be more transparent in its use of training data.

Central to any AI system is training data, **a lot** of training data. If you can't get access to this then you can't refine your models, the capabilities of your systems are reduced and the accuracy of your responses is degraded. This is a problem that we will look at in more detail in the training data section.

Key things:

- ChatGPT from OpenAI opened up the possibilities of AI to the world at large.
- They pioneered the use of chat prompting to develop a product that reached market first.
- The release of ChatGPT accelerated the push from the tech giants to release their own equivalent LLMs.
- OpenAI has a multitude of products, not just ChatGPT.

15: The Big Players in AI – Meta (Facebook)

Three billion and counting: I need users, lots of users.[23]

Another very big technology firm has moved to engage with and build products that are AI based.
Meta Platforms, the parent company taking in Facebook, Instagram and other key products such as WhatsApp, has made in the last two years a very large move from their Metaverse adventures, which has had mixed success, to AI ventures.

They have played to their strengths in AI, such as access to enormous data centres, tens of thousands of developers and a focus on user-centric design. As such, they have developed their own large language model, called Llama 2, which is described by Meta as a mix of pre-trained and fine-tuned models.

Meta claims that it has been trained on 40 per cent more data than the previous version and this is part of their AI 'secret sauce'. The advantage they have over every other AI player is users, lots of users. They can deploy the data that they have gleaned from their three billion-plus users of Facebook and Instagram. The harvesting of this data that is generated every day and the training of its models is a huge part of the Meta advantage.

Llama 2 is open source, you can download and make changes to it, for example feed it your own training data, you can't do this with ChatGPT. Also, there are claims that the performance of Llama is better than OpenAI's GPT; however, in tests it does appear that OpenAI is better at purely creative work, for example writing a poem.

[23] Paraphrasing *The Matrix*.

Meta is clearly trying to make their large language model ubiquitous through ease of access and the ability to modify it as needed. In addition, they are developing their own computer chips, focused on AI. These are called **MTIAs** (meta training and inference accelerator) chips. The design of these has been heavily weighted towards working with deep learning models. Remember that a key part of any language model is the ability to predict, or infer, the next word in a block of text.

I'll have chips with that ...

These chips are part of that process. The really clever part of these chips though is that they actually serve a double purpose: they can not only work very efficiently with training models (remember this is how large language models get better, they are fed huge amounts of data and their responses are calibrated and improved until they are ready for prime time) but also as actual AI chips, where they can infer (or guess according to the less charitable) the next word or sentence in a structure.

It should be noted that Meta has also invested hugely in purchasing chips from Nvidia as they scale up their own chip manufacturing capabilities. Part of their strategy is to reduce their reliance on Nvidia for chips, not least because demand for Nvidia chips is so high that having restricted supply could impact their own AI plans.

Meta has also invested hugely in AI data centres; with their experience already in working with very large data sets within the Facebook and Instagram families it wasn't a huge stretch to start working with their already available data as part of their learning models. Their AI data centres are designed to cluster large numbers of their AI specific chips together with a focus on large language model capabilities.

So, they have their own chips, they have the data, **a lot** of data, they have their own data centres and are building specific AI chips, and have developed their own large language models. What's next? It appears that their focus is on improving their own products through the addition of AI tools. For example, better recommendations within Facebook, the serving of very precisely targeted ads based on language learning models and more.

Mark Zuckerberg, Meta CEO, has stated that they are looking to focus on creating *'AI personas that can help people in a variety of ways.'* This will likely make its way into the chat technologies deployed in Facebook, Instagram and WhatsApp.

They also have their own image-generating capability, snappily titled **Make a Scene** which has a goal of creating images that are in theory more diverse than the images that they have been trained on already. In effect, moving towards a key goal of AI, true originality in output. This also means it is easier to create new and original training data to improve large language models. That is a good thing as it reduces costs and improves accuracy.

Key things:

- Facebook has data, cloud computing data centres and advanced LLMs that make them a very serious player in AI.
- They also have their own AI chip designs.
- It appears that they have pivoted from their push into AR (remember the metaverse?) and moved towards AI as a key part of their strategic goals.
- They are already a big player in the AI space, have invested billions in software and hardware and are rapidly becoming one of the most important technology companies in AI.

16: The Big Players in AI – Apple

'Think different.' – Apple ad campaign 1987

Amongst all the tech giants involved in AI innovations, Apple, on the surface at least, appears to be the least voluble about what they are doing and what their plans for using AI in their products are.

However, of the large companies it has made the most AI acquisitions, no fewer than twenty-one, since 2017. This compares to eleven from Microsoft for example. So, what are they up to? As an incredibly secretive company it is hard for outsiders to get a view; however, there do appear to be some logical steps involving AI that they could make. With a user base of over one billion iPhones sold in the last four years and a secure software ecosystem including the App store, the potential customer base is huge.

Apple has tried the smart assistant process before, with the not terribly successful Siri. This product has been hampered due to Apple's data protection and privacy laws, which is a core part of their offering, where users are confident their data is secure. However, not being able to see how users are interacting with your product and view the quality of the answers provided by Siri to them is a major issue. The other tech giants do not hamper their teams in this way. As a result, Siri is not seen as particularly good by users and has been the butt of jokes for many years.

This is at least partially the manner in which Siri operates, it uses a database of possible questions that may be asked and if it gets asked anything that isn't already in the database it's stumped. This is kind of the opposite of any large language model where a system is trained on the sort of questions it may be asked and has a much broader remit to respond.

Apple is keenly aware that its security model means that any AI system will need to adhere to data privacy rules. But what if you could have the AI language model run on your iPhone? The data never leaves the device; it's not shared with others and can respond to your requests in a far better way than Siri ever can. It is called edge computing (move the data from the centre to the edge, in this case the cell phone) and it isn't just Apple that has invested a lot of resources into this.

However, Apple has an entire ecosystem:

- Their own Operating Systems: **iOS**
- Their own hardware: **iPhones**
- Their own chips: **M1, M2s, M3s, M4s..**you get the picture
- Their own LLMs: **Ferret** (one of many)

They also have twenty-one companies specialising in AI, each with a different element to add to the AI whole. One example is Silk Labs an American AI company that developed security cameras that can recognise individuals. All of the computation is done on the camera itself and the imaged stored on the device. Very much in line with how Apple operates. And there are twenty more companies, all in the AI space, adding to the Apple family.

So with all of these elements the potential for Apple to capitalise on AI is enormous yet they appear to be a laggard in this race. At the time of publishing there were strong indications that Apple would link up with Google's Gemini generative AI model and integrate their technology into iPhone software. However, Apple have also been talking with OpenAI so the exact direction is unclear. Integrating either Gemini or ChatGPT LLMs into the iPhone would be a huge and potentially game-changing move for the 'also-ran'. At the moment, it appears there is still a focus on improving Siri and its responses.

Key things:

- Apple have it all AI-wise; however, they have yet to capitalise on their strengths.
- Apple are likely concerned about impacting their reputation for protecting their users' data by implementing AI that is trained on user data.
- On-device LLMs powered by Apple chips (iPhones, iPads and possibly more) would be incredibly important and would propel them higher up the list of true AI innovators.
- A link-up with Google or OpenAI could have massive implications for Apple in breaking through with their own AI solution enabled for the Apple ecosystem.

17: The Big Players in AI – Google

Surely, we can't do that. We can and don't call me Shirley ...[24]

If you were to set the foundations for the perfect (on paper) AI company then you would surely choose Google. There are quite a few reasons why ...

- It has AI embedded into its recommendation engines for YouTube, Gmail and its search algorithms.
- Google has unbelievable amounts of video, text and data from Youtube, Gmail and of course its search engine that can be used as training data.
- It has pretty much unlimited funds.
- It bought the ground-breaking AI start-up company DeepMind in 2014.
- It published a paper in 2017 that OpenAI itself cited as an important factor in its development of ChatGPT as it looked at more efficient ways to parse data.[25]
- It has published papers on the transformer model and other innovations in AI over many years since 2017.
- It has groundbreaking TensorFlow chips, essential for AI computing.
- It has its own highly developed cloud computing arm.
- It has one billion-plus users of the Android operating system for phones.

---

[24] ***Airplane***, statistically the funniest movie of all time.
[25] Parse as in to make data easier to understand, sometimes by converting from one format to another.

And yet they can't seem to catch a break. Their flagship AI model, Bard (now renamed Gemini), was over a year late and was rushed to release following enormous pressure in order to compete with ChatGPT, which had been released the previous year (2022). It's fair to say that the response to the Gemini LLM product has not been widely positive.

Some of the criticisms levelled against it included the fact that its answers were less complete than ChatGPT or Copilot, with some commentators reporting that Bard had the 'most bizarre'[26] answers of the three major chat engines. One of the more headlines generating issues was that the bias in Gemini was such that it had difficulty creating white characters or would create non-white individuals representing obviously white groups such as Vikings. This blew up in the media and had the likes of Elon Mush calling the system 'racist'.

None of this was a good look and demonstrated the perils of bias in large language models. The risk of moving too far in any one direction is real and with outputs available to anyone using the models feedback is swift and can be harsh. The backlash was such that Google paused image generation of individuals on Gemini while they looked at what could be done to address the issues found.

In addition, the responses generated for prompt questions were accused of left-wing bias, equating Elon Musk with Hitler while ChatGPT for example gave a definitive response stating, 'It isn't appropriate or accurate to compare them.'

And yet ... Google still has all of the advantages to make it an incredibly important player in AI. None of these advantages have gone away but they have failed in the execution. Like a

---

[26] Wired, Lauren Goode reporting.

machine learning model, it is expected that they learn from the errors made and improve the AI products that they offer. They can be expected to iterate and improve. Already they are looking at replacing Google Assistants on mobile devices with Gemini AI-enabled tools.

As a result, while we can't count Google out, they have made a lot of unforced errors, they clearly have issues with bias in their models and their marketing leaves a lot to be desired, for example where they skipped whole steps of their multimodal Gemini presentation to give a misleading impression of its capabilities.[27]

So Google are sort of the Microsoft of the AI era: the old Microsoft, that was late to smartphones, late to Cloud computing and late to browsers.

But in the end Microsoft won.....

---

[27] Look up Gemini AI model demonstration, called *Hands-on with Gemini: Interacting with multimodal AI* on, well, YouTube. It looks amazing, the problem is that the video isn't a real, seamless demo. Google stitched elements together. It was a shame as it would have been amazing if it really was that slick.

Key things:

- Like Meta and Apple, Google has huge advantages in AI.
- They haven't been able to capitalise on their advantages yet but have made errors in their anti-bias weightings that due to the size of Google have been very visible to the world.
- Gemini is the name of Google's flagship LLM (until they rename it again...you may have noticed a theme where AI players keep changing the name of their products...)

18: The Big Players in AI – Nvidia

The ultimate one-stop shop

We have looked at the major players in AI and there is one thing that they all have in common, namely that they all rely on one company to make their advances in AI. Namely Nvidia.

It is the eight-hundred-pound gorilla of the AI hardware world. Started as a company that focused on creating computer chips, called GPUs (graphics processing units), for the gaming industry in 1993 it has pivoted to making its products indispensable for **any** company wishing to capitalise on the AI boom.

The company's famed RTX chips are used to power the incredibly CPU-intensive demands that come with training large language models.

However, it is not just chip manufacturing that they are involved with, they have focused over many years on building out an entire AI ecosystem of software and related processes and technologies as well as chips. They have adapted, improved and out-competed all other chip manufacturers to become one of, if not the, most important players in AI.

This is not to say that the other big players don't have their own chips, Meta and Google for example have very sophisticated AI chip designs of their own; however, as of early 2024 Nvidia was estimated to have approximately 70 per cent of **all** AI chip sales.

- **Volta**: A chip designed for data centres, favoured for speed.
- **Tensor Cores**: These are, well, the core of Nvidia GPUs that massively increased the speed of calculations executed within LLMs.
- **GPUs**: Nvidia's own graphics processing units, optimised to parallel process, which means more calculations can be executed at the same time.
- **A100 and H100s**. These are the most expensive and most capable Nvidia chips. If you need LLM processing done at scale then you need these.
- **Xavier:** A chip designed for automotive AI, a good example of edge computing.

I'll have chips with that: some of the chips made by Nvidia:

In doing this they have made themselves central to AI research and improvements in the tech sector. Simply put, without them we would likely not have anywhere near the level of advancements that have been made in this space. One example is their pioneering work with transformer calculations.

These have traditionally been incredibly CPU intensive and to cater for this Nvidia produced their H100 chipset, specifically designed to handle these calculations. Technology breakthroughs such as these were a big part in enabling ChatGPT for example to create a working chat prompt model.

If we look at their different chips, they have a lot of different designs each focused on solving different AI problems as you can see in the table above. They have invested over $8 billion in chip design and manufacturing in 2024 (fiscal year) and there are no signs of this level of spending slowing down. None of these chips work in isolation, they need highly advanced software to operate as designed. There is a slew of different software platforms that have been developed, the most important ones are CUDA (this allows linking up GPUs to do the heavy lifting in AI models) and TensorRT, which allows companies to create their own deep learning models running on Nvidia chips. They have a lot more software (my favourite is Isaac, a software system developed for robots, it's pretty amazing) than this and without it their chips simply would not have the impact that they have had on the world.

Key things:

- Nvidia don't just make AI chips ...
- But they do make many different AI chip designs.
- Its software advances in AI are almost as important as its hardware advances.

Nvidia aims to be the leader in AI and it is doing a very good job of it.

19: AI Hardware

Beam me up, Scotty

Technologists tend to love science fiction. Science fiction in turn provides us with compelling narratives of what future technologies look like. One of the most well-known is the *Star Trek* Communicator that functions as a scanner, communication device, universal translator and more.
Now, AI is attempting to emulate some of the functions of the trusty Communicator, although we are a bit far off from having the transporter capabilities.

A number of approaches have been taken. One is to make a dedicated device, the other is to augment an existing one, usually a mobile phone. A recent example of a dedicated device is called the Rabbit R1, a small handheld device. The Rabbit is an interesting take on the AI model; it is a small, handheld device with a screen, a camera, speakers and a microphone. The user communicates with it and the device carries out the tasks assigned to it.

One use case is ordering food from a specific restaurant and asking the Rabbit to choose the most ordered item from the restaurant and have it delivered by 7 p.m. The device has a built-in AI model and clearly hit the right spot for early adopters, the first batch of ten thousand sold out within twenty-four hours of launch.

But surely you could do all of this on your existing mobile device without needing a separate device? That is what Apple, Samsung and Google are all banking on. Dedicated AI chips are now being incorporated into their latest generation devices, for example on the Samsung S24, as well as with the Apple A16 bionic chip in the latest iPhones.

The aim of these chips is to **maximise** processing speed, to deal with the huge computational needs of AI algorithms. These chips power elements such as facial recognition but the possibilities to extend into the use cases of devices such as the Rabbit R1 are clear.

Then there are the hybrid devices that are AI-enabled. Examples of these include the Oculus Rift from Meta (Facebook) and Apple's Vision Pro. These have AI built into them, the Vision Pro in particular uses edge computing (see Chapter 19 for more detail), which allows a lot of the AI functionality of the device to be processed locally. This really helps with features such as room mapping, so you don't fall over the nearest table, as well as tracking the movement of your eyes.

The biggest feature within these two devices is the building of virtual reality (in the case of the Oculus) and augmented reality (Vision Pro) worlds.[28] These are both heavily reliant on AI to make these experiences happen, not just eye tracking but also full understanding of where you are looking, the direction you are moving and the rendering of those images in as close to real time as possible.

---

[28] Virtual reality is an entire ecosystem that you are immersed in, you cannot interact with anything real in your vicinity. Augmented reality on the other hand allows you to see what is happening around you but overlaid with something else; for example, if you work as a maintenance engineer you could see a technical diagram overlaid on the jet engine you may be working on.

The result is that we are far more likely to see AI-**enabled** devices rather than AI devices that are built specifically with the aim of having AI capabilities. After all, your phone can still make and take calls as well as recognise faces.

Due to the sheer size and importance of Nvidia it has its own section, see Chapter 18. Remember that GPU chips are the heart of any AI system. The Nvidia chapter will break this down in more detail.

Key things:

- There are dedicated AI hardware devices, such as the Rabbit.
- A more widely adopted approach for AI integration into hardware is into devices we already own, such as cell phone, smart TVs and while there are more specific dedicated AI home devices such as Amazon's Alexa products.
- Devices that learn and optimise themselves based on your routine are already becoming the norm, with more AI integration they will become even more ubiquitous.
- Don't forget the GPUs, these are the chips that enable the massive processing capabilities required by AI.

20: AI and Edge Computing

Life on the edge

One of the buzzwords of the last few years has been edge computing. This is where instead of having data centres doing all the heavy lifting when you are doing computing heavy tasks, such as face recognition or augmented reality you push all that computing work to the edge, to your actual device. That's pretty much it. For most of us, our phones are the first devices to show edge computing at work with AI. For example, the Samsung S24 has AI features such as live translations,[29] generative AI to edit your photos and AI summaries of notes that you have created on the device.

As phones become more powerful, they can run the very intensive tasks that AI requires. The other device that benefits massively from edge computing are connected cars, Tesla, Mercedes Benz and BYD are paving the way in this area.

The massive advantage of edge computing, doing your AI processing on the device itself, is to reduce latency, or slowness, that would result if inputs, for example camera images, had to be processed in a data centre and the resulting actions then returned to the device. Having onboard computation in a car means that instant decisions can be executed, such as braking suddenly to avoid a person stepping into the road or making a turn safely, taking into account all the traffic in the area.

---

[29] The live translation app allows near real-time communication on calls between you and someone speaking another language. It's quite remarkable although there are times when the latency(slowness) does result in minor confusion.

As well as speed, the advantages of edge computing for AI include real-time tracking of speed of process flow, for example in a factory. Issues on an automated line can be tracked instantly, for example by cameras, and AI algorithms can then adjust and potentially resolve these issues.

In retail, Walmart uses AI machine learning processes, tied to input systems such as sensors and cameras, to manage inventory more effectively. This is edge computing at work. Inventory management in retail is incredibly important and often a source of competitive advantage. If you get it wrong, either under- or over-ordering you can go very bust, very fast.

So, the Walmart systems constantly monitor inventory levels in enormous distribution centres. However, unlike standard camera systems, these systems learn the levels, the trends and the shifts in demand and act upon this data to reorder stock as required. As more and more data are gathered and inventory is ordered the accuracy of this reordering is adjusted by the machine learning algorithms and constantly improved.

This is only a small part of AI models used by Walmart. With their access to huge data sets showing buyer behaviour, the company claims that it can differentiate demand for items down to specific zip codes. This means that they can position items with a very high degree of confidence.

However, security breaches with edge computing and AI are a

very real concern. With systems so closely linked to hardware actions, such as steering a car, the potential for hackers to inflict damage is a real risk.

Key things:

- Edge computing in AI looks to move the processing of large data sets and the use of algorithms towards the device itself and away from large data centres.
- A more widely adopted approach for AI integration into hardware will be into devices we already own, such as cell phone, smart TVs and home devices such as Amazon's Alexa products.
  Devices that learn and optimise themselves based on your routine are already becoming the norm, with more AI integration they will become more capable and ubiquitous.

21: Do Androids Dream of Electric Sheep?

'I never said most of the things I said.' – Yogi Berra

Sometimes AI systems do dream, or at least sometimes have problems separating facts from reality. We call these **hallucinations** and they can cause no end of problems and we can break these problems into three broad categories:

1. **Getting stuff wrong**. An example would be a vision recognition system that thinks a white truck on the road is actually a stop sign.

2. **Demonstrating bias and being potentially discriminatory**. There have been cases of AI facial recognition systems struggling with identifying people of colour.

3. **Flat out making stuff up**. We have numerous examples of AI systems making up entirely fictitious legal cases, which were then used by lawyers as supporting evidence for court cases. You can imagine the response of the judge to that one...

All of these are referred to as **hallucinations**, carrying over from the field of human psychology to the realm of computer science. Meta has a marvellous term for it: *'confident statements that are not true'*. This was in the context of concerns with one of their earlier AI models called **Galactica** that had a knack for citing scientific papers that did not exist, according to Ars Technica. Ars had a pithier description, they said it *'could generate realistic nonsense'*.[30] This system was so inaccurate that it was pulled by Microsoft.

Now it should be noted that **every** software system **ever** invented has bugs that are corrected by developers in a short period. No system is **ever** perfect upon release, it needs multiple iterations to get it right and this rule applies equally to AI systems. Every version change addresses existing bugs and often introduces a bunch of new ones![31]

But why do AI systems have a tendency to hallucinate? All of the major players in this field have ploughed hundreds of millions into researching these problems and there is a broad consensus that the root causes of this problem lie with:

- **Training data**: it may be unrepresentative of the domain it is being asked to work within. It may be biased; for example, the facial recognition systems may have been largely trained using one particular group of individuals, for example white males, leaving the system confused when presented with an image of a Hispanic woman for example.

- **Overfitting**: This is what happens when AI systems are trained using training data and perform brilliantly, but only with that specific training data. When presented with **new** data it has big problems. In effect it has memorised the training data rather than understood the **patterns** in that data, a crucial distinction. Don't forget that the key to a highly performant AI system is

30 *New Meta AI demo writes racist and inaccurate scientific literature, gets pulled* | **Ars Technica.**

31 Have a look at my book *"The 2 Minute Tester"* for some of the **many ways** software development can go wrong.

the ability to work with data that it has not encountered before. Overfitting is where the system's focus is on the wrong areas.

- AI systems often hallucinate because they simply don't have **enough** data to answer the question that has been asked and programmatically have issues stating that fact, that is, I don't know the answer.

So, what can be done to stop AI systems from hallucinating? There are a large number of ways to stop systems from hallucinating and they are very much focused on:

- **The quality of the data**
- **The quantity of the data**
- **How the system learns from the data**

Let's look at some ways to stop AI from making stuff up:

1. The first way is the most technically straightforward way, having a **human in the loop**. This means that humans actually find and correct the hallucinations as they occur. For example, imagine you have a large language model trained on case law and during the course of its training every so often it produces a case that simply never occurred. The human in the loop would flag this as an incorrect and invalid response and that is recognised by the algorithm. This method is very time-consuming and hallucinations suffer from a randomness paradox, triggering a hallucination is not linear. So, this process helps but it's not perfect.

2. The second way is to **throw dodgy[32] data at the learning model**. This is called adversarial training and it attempts to introduce data that the AI system will accept as genuine but isn't. In essence, it tries to trick the AI into making incorrect predictions, hence the term adversarial. It's a very interesting approach that OpenAI amongst others have done a lot of work on.

Remember that we have discussed multimodal AI in previous chapters (the *ability to work with images, text, sound and code),* well we can take that approach to preventing, or limiting, hallucinations.

If we take images first. Imagine that we have one thousand images, all of rabbits. However, we manipulate a certain number, say fifty of those images, and add them to the overall training data of one thousand images. We may have only changed one pixel in each of the fifty images but they have been changed nonetheless. We then train the model with this data set, looking for it to capture and identify the manipulated images.

We can do the same with sound files. We may have a system designed to recognise and then change spoken words into text instantly, across twenty different languages. Once we have reached a certain level of competency, we now need to make it much harder, in other words adversarial.

So, we can inject random noises into the sound files used for training—they could be traffic sounds, other people talking, radios in the background—until the model still operates at a high level. Amazon Alexa still manages to hear

---

[32] **'Dodgy'** in this instance refers to unusual or random pieces of data.

your voice over the television, the dog barking and the doorbell ringing, that is the result of a lot of adversarial training!

It is an effective approach to reduce hallucinations but it does require a lot of computing power and also can slow down the processing time to give accurate results.

3. **Get better and more data**. This one sound easy. Your AI system is showing bias, OK, let's train it with unbiased data. But what defines unbiased data? How do you get more representative data? This is a hot topic in AI and is not as easy to solve as it appears at first glance. You can oversee the data that is being used by the learning algorithms and look for bias in that data. The system then improves based on this feedback. This sounds great.

The problem is that you need a lot of humans when you have a lot of data. At some point your data set is going to get so big you simply can't scale the human oversight. However, for small, specific data sets this is a proven method.

However, at least the issue of unrepresentative data is recognised now as an issue in contributing to hallucination issues in AI systems. This is also an area where having a human in the loop really makes a difference (assuming of course that this person isn't biased) to assist the process.

4. We have some other approaches as well, one is called the **ensemble**[33] method. Remember that a key part of any AI system is predicting what the next word will be in a

[33] Remembering that *ensemble* is French for "together" makes it easier to understand.

sentence if you are working with a text prompt AI. So, if you combine a bunch of different AI models together, surely you will get a better quality of answer as they will have been trained on different data models and programmed differently? It's a solid response and does help.

An analogy is with aeroplane systems these days. You have a primary computer system that flies the plane, if the parameters appear incorrect the aeroplane will switch to a secondary (and a third and there is even a fourth on most modern airliners) to keep flying. In AI, if you have many different models all telling you that that picture of a stop sign is 99.98 per cent certainly a stop sign then you have taken a lot of the risk away.

But, and it's a big but, you do need a lot of computing power to do this and you have to integrate all of these different models together. This is not a trivial task by any stretch of the imagination.

There are further technical approaches to addressing the hallucination issue; however, what is likely to be the most effective is a **layered approach**. That is, combining two or more of the tactics described to reduce hallucinations to a low level. The end goal of entirely eliminating hallucinations is unlikely to be achievable in the near future, given the vagaries of data sets, humans and systems so all AI providers are working to reduce to an acceptable level.

Key things:

- AI systems love to make stuff up sometimes, this is called hallucinating.
- There are multiple causes of hallucinations.
    - Poor data
    - Lack of data
    - Overfitting
    - Semantic leaps (this is where AI logic makes a logic jump and makes an incorrect inference)
- I prefer the term 'making stuff up' to hallucinations.

22: Dangers of AI, Fraud and More ...

'More human than human.' – Tyrell, *Blade Runner*, 1982

The capabilities of AI that make it so powerful mean that inevitably, just like the internet, it can be used for negative outcomes. The ability to impersonate individual's voices and appearances means that the more common tools that financial institutions use to identify customers are under threat.

In one case an individual in 2023 was tricked by fraudsters to wire $25 million of his company's money to a scammer's account. The fraudsters had used AI to create deepfake images of key leaders in his company including the company's CFO. He dialled into a video call with them and was put at ease as he saw and interacted with them and so authorised the transfer. The money wasn't seen again.[34]

Deepfakes are becoming more prevalent and more convincing. They are AI-generated outputs that are manipulated to imitate an individual's image, voice or video. They are a serious security risk for you as an individual being impersonated in order to defraud you as well as for those in the media whose words can be manipulated for scam purposes, for example, selling products that they aren't associated with in any way.

Areas that are most at risk from deepfake creation using generative AI are:

Disinformation: Manipulated images of candidates widely shared on social media are likely to pose a very big risk to fair election results. Large state actors such as China and Russia have well-developed capabilities in this area and are likely to

---

[34] The finance officer believed he was talking to Hong Kong-based colleagues on a video call.

deploy such tools in order to benefit their agendas.

Financial fraud: Impersonation risk, voice cloning using deepfake technology is getting very accurate. Sometimes referred to as deepfake audio.

Identity theft: Not just financial fraud but wider creation of 'synthetic media' resulting in massive intellectual property theft with negative impacts on copyright and creator rights.

The way in which deepfakes are created is that a neural network, as part of the broader deep learning technique, takes existing images, sounds or videos of a person and trains a model to create new output based on those inputs. The more data it has to train on the more accurate it is likely to be. As we covered earlier in the chapter on generative AI principles, the neural network that creates deepfakes relies on two elements: the **generator** and the **discriminator** as a **GAN (general adversarial network)**.

They work in competition with each other, with the generator attempting to create output such that the discriminator cannot discriminate the generated output. Once that is achieved, typically very quickly, you have your deepfake image, video or voice output.

Until recently, the logic and computing power required to create deepfakes was out of reach for most individuals, due to cost and computing power demands. Now, with the latest generative AI models anyone can create a form of deepfakes and post the results on social media.

The large tech companies in this area have attempted to put strict guardrails around the creation and dissemination of deepfakes. They are purposefully vague about the exact methods they use to identify what has sometimes been called 'inauthentic' information but it is clear that there is an arms race to create undetectable manipulated imagery.

Microsoft's Copilot states in its rules that '*The model is designed to refuse harmful requests and prioritize safety*'. Meta (Facebook) has a blanket deepfake ban not dissimilar to X (formerly Twitter) advising that they will reduce the visibility of doctored images or videos.

There are a number of ways that AI is used to make fraud easier:

1. **Deepfakes**: video images that convincingly imitate an individual and are manipulated to say or do something this person would never do.

2. **Voice cloning**: AI tools don't require many words from an individual to very convincingly copy a person's voice. Authentication phone calls for banking are thus made much riskier. There has been a big rise in people receiving phone calls from panicked relatives asking for urgent money transfers. Needless to say, their son or daughter's voices have been cloned and the money is lost.

3. **Old-fashioned spam emails or messages**. Traditionally spam emails or messages via social media have been easy to spot, misspellings as well as awkward phrasing giving the game away. However, with ChatGPT these messages can be cleaned up, made to read very convincingly and generally sound more plausible.

All of these also apply to election influencing, making candidates voice opinions that they would never normally do. The social media giants are fighting a running battle with state actors as well as fraudsters to identify and remove malicious AI content on their platforms. Meta has advised that they are using specific pattern recognition processes, identifiers of content created using their own language model (llama) to root out AI-generated content.

Other efforts are at the standards level; an initiative called C2PA (Coalition for Content Provenance and Authenticity) is a planned standard that will in theory allow anyone to confirm that what they are looking at is genuine. This uses cryptographic standards, like a digital watermark or hologram, not visible to the human eye but visible in the metadata of an image. This watermark lets the user know whether the image has been created by AI or by a human.

OpenAI introduced this in Dall-E, their image creator; however, it is not yet widespread and may not be adopted by all of the tech companies, but this or something similar is likely to gain traction as identity fraud or impersonation becomes worse.

This is, however, an ongoing technical arms race, as the technology companies target AI-created content, new ways of subverting them constantly appear, for example using different language models.

From your perspective there are some things that you can do to protect yourself from AI scams, some of them are common sense, others more technical.

1. **Go random**: You get a video or phone call from a colleague at work. Normally AI-generated systems will follow a specific train of conversation so if you are not 100 per cent sure it is that person then ask them a random, unrelated question and see how they respond.

2. **Trust your instincts**: Does the voice match the images exactly? We've all seen poorly dubbed movies and very quickly we spot that something is off. Look at the hands if you can, AI finds creating authentic-looking hands a challenge, and there have been instances of more than five fingers being visible on deepfake videos. The human brain is superb at spotting the smallest of differences, look at movies where they have used AI to recreate actors who have died. You know almost instantly it is them, but not quite them. This is called the '*uncanny valley*' and you should use it in your attempts to keep yourself safe.

3.**Trust your instincts (again)**: Fraudsters rely on speed, they try to push you to make quick decisions so that your critical instincts are impaired. Think about what you are being asked to do, does it make sense? Are they asking you not to discuss this with anyone else?

4. **Have a good look at the background**: If it is a video, AI-generated personas are very good; however, lighting, tone and general background images are often a giveaway that something is not quite right. Does something look not quite right? If so, dig deeper.

There are also tools that are available that allow you to identify AI content. They tend to focus on different AI areas, such as text. For example, GPTZero is proving very popular with educators in spotting plagiarism or flat-out ChatGPT-created content.

Reality Defender and Deepware Scanner are very popular in assessing video content while Google's SynID is focused on artwork and images. New tools are being rolled out all the time that fight to keep the fraudsters at bay.

Key things:

- AI can be used as a tool for fraud in examples such as deepfakes, voice cloning and spam creation.
- In order to counter the risk of being taken in by AI-generated fraud look at following these steps:
    - Inject randomness into any communications, AI-generated systems look to follow pre-defined paths with questions and answers.
    - Look at backgrounds, hands and voice syncing with images. Look for mismatches or inconsistencies.
    - Slow down, make decisions at your own speed, don't be rushed.
    - Look at anti-fraud tools.

23: Visions of an AI Future – School's Out

An AI-enabled classroom

Millie sat down at her desk, tapped a small button on the side of her glasses and spoke: '*Start French Lesson 4, In the Café.*' The room around her faded away, and projected on to her eyes was the interior of a Parisian Cafe, filled with people chatting away and she found herself sitting at an ornate table.

As she moved her hands a menu appeared in them and she was able to read the different items. Once she had chosen, she gestured to the waiter who came over, smiled and asked, '*Oui, mademoiselle*?'

She smiled and said, '*Bonjour, une café s'il vous plait,*' the waiter smiled again and said, '*Bien sur,*' and moved away to fetch her coffee. *Hmm, those cakes look good* she thought, *when he comes back, I'll order one too…*

While all of this was visible in her field of vision, she could also just about see the outline of her own bedroom, her desk and her cat that was still fast asleep on a cushion in the corner.

All of this (apart from a Parisian waiter actually smiling) is likely to be possible within a short time frame thanks to AI technologies. If we look at the near future of the Apple Pro headset and combine that technology with sophisticated machine learning systems, we could all learn a new language in any country that we choose.

Overall, Education is likely to become far more **personalised**, **interactive** and **adaptive**. If we focus on personalisation, the capacity to tailor learning based on the outcomes of previous lessons is a very powerful tool in itself.

Educators today struggle to find the time to provide that one-on-one focus in a classroom of twenty or thirty students. AI can, though, adjusting learning based on the strengths and weaknesses of periodic testing and presenting material as it relates to improving that student's progress. So, in that wider class of students, while the theme has been set by the teacher, each student may be focusing on a slightly different aspect of the topic that matches their learning style.

Specifically, AI learning systems will adapt the difficulty of a lesson in real time, something you may see already in apps such as the language learning app Duolingo, which present you with more or less challenging phrases depending on your previous answers.

AI is **not** going to replace teachers; rather they will benefit from AI systems that will not only support each student but provide the teacher with constant analysis and tracking of which students need the most support and how they are progressing as a class. This will extend to marking and grading of work, even where students need to write answers. To put this into context, an AI-enabled classroom will free the teacher from the lower value tasks such as grading and will give them more time for creativity in their teaching approaches.

The interactive element is going to mean more VR[35] and AR options for students. Whether it is manipulating virtual molecules, constructing mechanical models or choosing the right way to order a meal in Cantonese, the world of learning will be made much richer.

---

[35] VR: virtual reality, AR: augmented reality.

One of the greatest benefits of AI in the classroom will be to assist students with disabilities, those who struggle with reading text would have real-time audio for any text while those who have problems with writing would benefit hugely from AI dictation possibilities. Thus, different learning modes will be supported through AI to the benefit of students.

With all of these opportunities the boundaries of a classroom will become more blurred. The very real shortcomings of distance learning experienced by students during Covid-19 lockdowns concentrated minds on what was needed to improve teaching that occurred outside a physical classroom.

Zoom calls really didn't cut it as students struggled to engage and feel part of a wider group in an effective manner. Tools such as AR and VR will support these efforts, and having your own personal education assistant, guiding and helping you on your learning journey, all while having the expertise of trained teachers means that education will be more fulfilling and engaging for both educators and students.

Key things:

- AI will act as a hugely helpful enabler to teachers. Teachers aren't going anywhere.
- The ability to stay on top of standard classroom administration, such as student progress monitoring, weakness identification and curriculum advice and support means that AI will be the ultimate classroom assistant.
- Freeing up teachers to, well, teach is the gift that AI will bring to the classroom.

24: Visions of an AI Future – On the Road (and in the Air)

Martha looked up, her communicator bleeped and a voice in her ear spoke. '*Your vehicle has arrived. It is ten minutes early as the traffic on the route is slightly heavier than usual.*' She gulped down her coffee, shouldered her backpack and made for the car.

As she approached the car its door opened and she got in. She settled herself in and the vehicle started on its journey to the airport, silently and with a minimum of fuss. There was no driver, indeed there was no steering wheel. The car made its way through the small Italian village where she lived and joined the main autostrada towards Milan, merging seamlessly with the traffic.

Driverless trucks passed by, often in convoys, with only one-meter separation between each one, taking advantage of the slipstream effect to maximise energy efficiency. Regular cars passed by, the majority not being driven by their owners, with un-Italian-like adherence to speed limits and road rules.

The few cars that were being manually driven were given a wider berth by autonomous vehicles, their sensors advising that reaction times would be slower and that the risk of accidents higher, so stay clear.

As her vehicle approached a set of traffic lights they moved from red to green as beside her car a driverless coach had drawn alongside. Matching the coach's speed meant that Martha's car would not have to wait at any lights; sensors in the coach as well as camera systems in the traffic lights meant that any public transport vehicles had as smooth a journey as possible.

She soon arrived at the drop-off zone at Milan airport. Getting out of the car, her glasses showed on the left lens a small green arrow indicator for her to follow to the bag drop-off area. She smiled, just enough time for another coffee!

The way we get around, by car, train, plane or ship, will be hugely impacted by artificial intelligence.
The profusion of lidar[36] and camera sensors, neural networked systems and integrated traffic systems means that the overall safety levels of travel will rise greatly.

Adoption rates will be uneven, in the developed world in clearly mapped, predictable travel routes such as highways AI systems embedded in vehicles will be ubiquitous. In less structured environments such as cities in the developing world the capabilities of AI-enabled driving systems will be reduced and will take far longer to be adopted.

Elon Musk has predicted fully autonomous driver experiences since 2016 for Tesla, each of these deadlines blasted by with no sign of fully self-driving vehicles. Reacting to other vehicles, reading road markings, adjusting speed and overtaking are all difficult enough. Add to the mix unpredictable pedestrians, navigating roundabouts, common in the UK, France and Australia to name a few, is another level of difficulty.

We haven't yet reached the point of fully autonomous driving systems that can function without any human intervention at all, level 5, but at the rate of advances in visual models, learning

---

[36] A form of radar that builds a three-dimensional view of the world.

from millions of miles of driver journeys and better computation it is going to happen, the big unknown is when.

It is useful to consider AI algorithms as providing the plumbing for the future of transport. It's really important but rarely visible to you. And, just like plumbing, you only notice it when it goes wrong.

One of the biggest advances will be in safety, not just driving safety by reducing the number of human errors, but also in terms of journey planning, avoiding hazardous routes due to poor weather conditions, traffic conditions as well as making it cost-efficient. Google's journey planner, bundled as part of Android Auto, uses AI to constantly assess these and other factors to optimise your journey.

In aviation, where autopilot systems have been in operation for many decades to reduce pilot workload, the next stage, enabled by AI, is coming close. The European aircraft manufacturer Airbus has been trialling its **DragonFly** concept. This enables the aircraft to identify features in the landscape, enabling the plane to fly itself in conditions that normally put high pressure on flight crews, such as a last-second go-around or diversion.

This also takes the concept of auto-land to the next level. Where weather conditions are poor current aircraft can have auto-land engaged, this lands the aircraft; however, pilot intervention is normally required to reverse the engine thrust to bring the aircraft to a stop. The Dragonfly concept not only lands the aircraft but also slows down and taxis the aircraft to the gate.

With such a system, built with multiple redundancies so that if one system fails another will take its place, the days of two pilots flying aircraft are likely to be numbered. One pilot should be able to monitor and intervene as needed. The key reasons for needing two pilots, such as flying workload, making radio calls and backing each other up in case of a medical event start to fade away with an AI-enabled aircraft. Just like Level 5 driving, the timelines around single or even no pilot aircraft are very uncertain.

Key things:

- AI should make travel a lot safer.
- Adoption rates will be heavily impacted by suitability of infrastructure as well as regulators willingness to permit usage of such technology.
- Flying will become even safer.

25: Visions of an AI Future – Popcorn Time

In 2023, from July to November, actors and writers went on strike. They had concerns not only about rates of pay but also about the rise of generative AI, specifically its ability to reuse actors' physical likenesses as well as their voices, to create brand-new content. [37]

The strike brought to the forefront fears about how AI could negatively impact the creative industries. Fears that movie studios would scan actors' likenesses, pay them for that day and then reuse their likenesses in any future movies that they created without paying them again.

The strike was resolved with the studios agreeing that they

must ask for consent forty-eight hours before they attempted to create a digital twin or replica of an actor (this also covered using their voice) and that the actor must be paid for the creation of the digital replica. There was also an agreement that if the studios used an actor's likeness to create a new digital actor, the actor would be compensated.

Similar issues with generative AI were raised by writers' guilds, specifically about the use of ChatGPT and similar tools to create and modify scripts. This was again resolved with guardrails put around the use of AI.[38]

However, the writing is on the wall, the creative industries are being upended by AI. When real-time videos can be created in seconds, screenplays generated without the need for

---

[37] The SAG-AFTRA strike as well as the Writer's Guild Association (WGA) were involved.
[38] The exact terms of what was agreed aren't in the public domain.

screenwriters and music can be composed without the need for musicians then what does that mean for those who currently work in the creative arts?

There is the perspective that they can use AI as a collaborative tool, for example a scriptwriter could use generative AI to draft an outline of a screenplay, then use their skills to refine and flesh out the specific details of it. This could equally apply to music, with the artist then refining what has been produced.

The AI giants are realising the impacts of their training models being used to create music, text and images in the style of a specific (living) artist. Version 3 of DALL-E has specific guardrails in place that won't let you create a picture in the style of an artist or author.

If you are a studio, you are likely to look at generative AI as a cost-saving option. Why employ ten screenwriters if you can get the same level of output from two using generative AI? The Studios do need take into account other factors, not least quality control and originality from AI generated output.

AI video and image generation systems are already unlocking enormous creativity from artists working with only a laptop, these are likely to pose a bigger risk to established studios as they now have a way of showcasing their output for free to millions. Just upload to YouTube....

Key things:

- Generative AI is a threat to those who work in the creative industries, most notably the movies.
- It is likely that in the near future we will have cinematic releases of movies created using AI that star our favourite actors who have licensed their images to be used.
- The result of this is that the overall cost of creating nominally original content is likely to fall, well, dramatically.
- Such changes will encounter resistance from those whose livelihoods depend on creating new content.

26: Getting Started in AI – Beginner

If you have no experience at all in AI the first thing you need to do is to experiment with it.
Let's start with writing a story and then creating an image to accompany that story using generative AI.

The easiest way of doing this is to choose an AI tool. If you already have Microsoft Edge browser on your computer then by default you will have access to Copilot, their AI tool. It can be found in the top right of the screen but is likely to become more embedded in the browser itself in time.

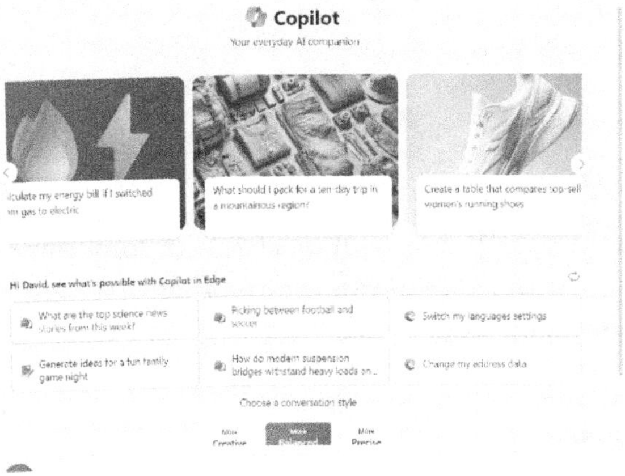

Fig 1: Microsoft Copilot

Or, if you prefer you can use ChatGPT (this is very quickly done, simply choose a username and a password). You then get a choice of using ChatGPT or their API generation tool, simply select ChatGPT and you are in.

If you choose the paid version of ChatGPT then you will get the most up-to-date version, faster processing and priority access.

You don't need to use that version, however; the free version is accessible too and is fine for getting started with AI and getting it to create a story for you.[39]

Fig 1: ChatGPT (this is version 3.5)

The next step is to then ask the AI solutions to write something for you. If you are using MS Copilot you can see that there are three (self-explanatory) options:

- **More Creative**
- **More Balanced**
- **More Precise**
-

If you are using ChatGPT you don't have these options, you just have a prompt box where you type in your command or what is called a chat prompt.

In the prompt area you have the following:

[39] At the time of writing, 2025, GPT4 is the paid for version.

Copilot

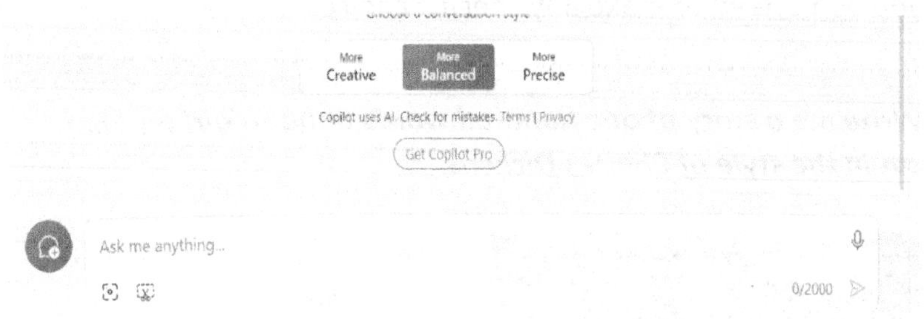

ChatGPT

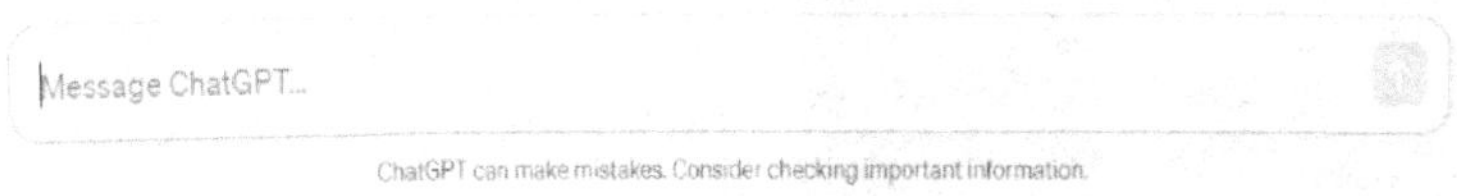

Type the following:

What is the length of the Mississippi River?

If you are using ChatGPT it will advise 2,320 miles long, if you use Copilot, it will advise 2,340 miles long. What gives? Even with such a standardised question as this you can see that solely relying on generative AI for factual data needs to be done carefully.

As discussed in earlier chapters, generative AI **cannot** be trusted 100 per cent of the time to give you an accurate answer, stuff will get made up, you need to do your own research, they even tell you this at the bottom of the chat prompt windows.

Story time

The next step is to use generative AI to create us a story. If you are using Copilot select the 'More Creative' option, in ChatGPT you don't need to make any specific choice.

Write me a story of one hundred words about a girl and her cat in the style of Charles Dickens

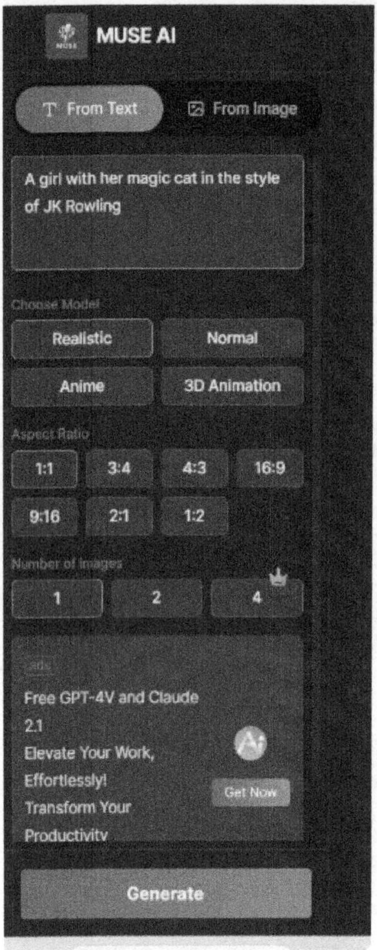

Both of them should, in the space of seconds, create a story for you. It is very likely that snow, London and characters with rather absurd names will feature heavily! As the machine learning models have been trained on the output of Charles Dickens, namely all his books, specific phrases, themes and tones will be used to imitate his style. You can then ask the AI models to add characters, create new worlds and more. With creative work such as this, if you are content with it, you can keep going. [40]

Image time

The next step is to create an image to go alongside our story. For this we will use Midjourney. We will use a

[40] As Charles Dickens' works are in the public domain, most, if not all, AI models are likely to have been trained on his writings. Newer authors, whose works are proprietary, are less likely to have their style accurately replicated by AI.

similar prompt to our story, tweaked slightly. So, look up Midjourney,[41] get registered and in the text, field type the following.

A girl with her magic cat

You do have specific options, such as Realistic, Normal, Anime or 3D Animation. Options for aspect ratio are also available.

Select Realistic, 1:1 Aspect Ratio and Number of Images: 1.

You are more limited with Midjourney compared to gen AI text tools as there is a limit on the number of images you can create (you do get more with the paid versions), which is down to the cost of generating images such as these. Image creation is processor heavy, using what are called convolutional neural networks (CNNs), which typically use more powerful chips.

[41] I refrain from using specific links as these change all the time. Just use your browser and search on the keywords, Midjourney, ChatGPT or Copilot.

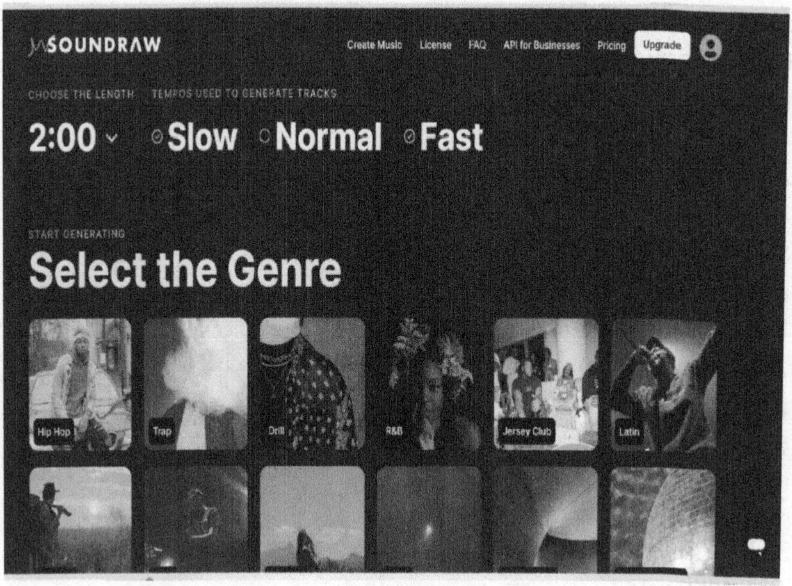

After clicking Generate your image should appear in seconds. Note that AI tools are now much clearer about the risks of using living artists or author's work and with the example above DALL-E (an image generator released by OpenAI, will not let you specify 'in the style of JK Rowling'. This is likely to change further as artists and authors look to opt out of their works being used to train machine learning models.

Music time

For the final piece of our creative output we will use AI to create a song to accompany the story and the picture we have already created. Look up Soundraw (or just Google AI-generated songs) and register to use the system. Select the length of the song (I chose two minutes), the genre (I chose ambient) and finally the tempo (normal). Within a few seconds I had no less than fifteen different song options created. Within a few seconds I had no less than fifteen different song options created. Select any of the songs created and press play. You can change the beats per minute, the instruments and more. When you are happy you can download your song. It's that easy.

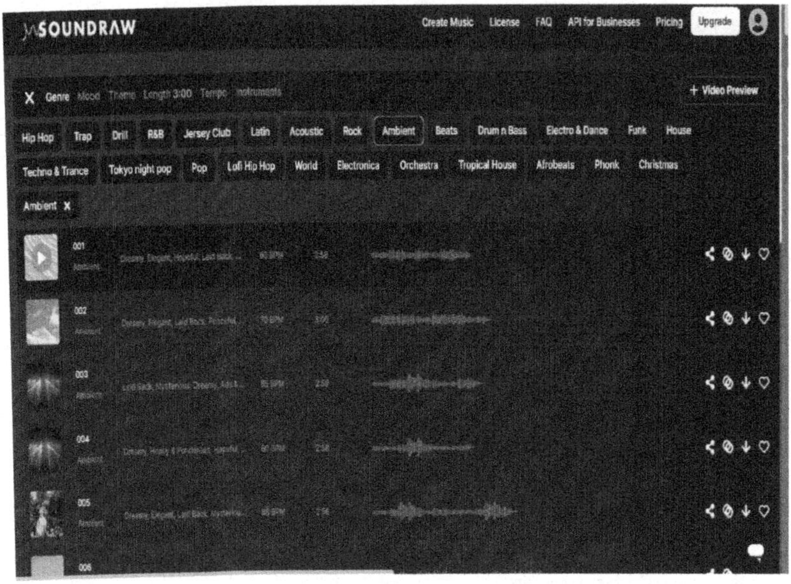

Key things:

- The best way to understand AI is to get hands-on with tools such as ChatGPT or Copilot.
- Have a go at writing a story, creating an image or a song.
- Experiment, experiment, experiment!
- When you are comfortable with these first steps then look at the next chapter and take it to the next level.

27: Getting Started in AI – Intermediate Level

With a little bit of prompting – the rule of six

Once you are familiar with accessing generative AI tools the next stage is to get a deeper understanding of prompt engineering, the science behind getting the best possible results out of generative AI.

There are specific principles that OpenAI and Microsoft recommend for getting the most out of ChatGPT or Copilot. As always, the best approach is to look at the guidelines and apply them to a specific task you would like to get done, for example improving an email, updating a story or creating a new recipe, it's up to you.

We can distil these rules into what we call the rule of six.

1. **Don't be vague:**

   Write me a nice poem about flowers.

   With a description like that, the results aren't going to be pretty, have a look at the first four lines:

   In gardens kissed by dawn's first light,
   Where petals bloom, a vibrant sight.
   A tapestry of colours, bold,
   Whispers tales of stories old.

   Instead, be specific:

Write me a four-line rhyming poem about spring flowers with colourful metaphors.

In April's embrace, the tulips sway,
Like paintbrush strokes in a vibrant ballet.
Daisies bloom, a field of white delight,
Springtime's palette, a floral flight.

Better, although sway and ballet is a bit clunky ...

2. **Use the latest AI models if possible. Paid versions will be the best.**
   It goes without saying that you should try to use the latest version of AI tools if you can. These are usually the paid versions, for example OpenAI tend to charge for their most recent versions, and will yield you the best results. Older AI models will fail to give you the best results, no matter how much you refine your prompts.

3. **Use separators if you are using ChatGPT (you don't need this with other AI tools)**
   Separators are symbols that help an AI system to understand what you need it to do and what sort of data, text or images you are providing it in your prompt. They can be ==== or #### or """".

   For example: *Write a two-sentence summary of the following paragraph.* ==== **The impact of asteroids on the demise of the dinosaurs is a subject of great debate. What is known is that the impact crater in what is now Mexico, would have been created by a meteorite measuring at least a mile wide and weighing at least a million tons. The resulting impact would**

have led to massive global disruption, with earthquakes, tsunamis and billions of tons of ash and dust filling the air. With the sun's rays obscured by this dust there would have been a rapid decline in temperatures, impacting the dinosaurs and their food sources. Within a few years it's likely that their population numbers would have plummeted====

A huge meteorite hit the Earth about sixty-six million years ago and caused a mass extinction of the dinosaurs. The impact triggered global cooling, natural disasters, and loss of habitats and food for the dinosaurs.

4. **Iterate, iterate, iterate.**
   If you aren't happy with the output created have a look at changing your prompt question structure, add or remove words, go specific as you can.

5. **Help it with examples**
   Prompts work extremely well if given an example to work with.

   Write four more sentences following the style, structure and theme of this poem==== In gardens kissed by dawn's first light, Where petals bloom, a vibrant sight.====

6. **Feedback helps**

   You can reuse the responses that you get from your AI tool to improve your overall result. If you ask it to write a speech about the merits of electric cars and you want to improve it you can take the speech generated and tell the system to make it less generic, focus on battery range and so on.

Doing this helps to refine the output more efficiently as you aren't starting from scratch every time. There are limits to this though, it won't retain a long-term memory unless you are training or tuning an LLM which is quite unlikely at this stage.

Key things:

- Don't be vague, go specific.
- For the best results use the paid versions.
- Use separators if using ChatGPT (it's not mandatory but can help)
- Iterate, a lot ...
- Give it examples to work with.
- Give it feedback.

28: Getting Started in AI – Going Deeper

You now have a solid understanding of the underlying principles of artificial intelligence. To go deeper you need to think about what specific area of AI you want to explore further. Do you want to focus on deep learning, neural networks, natural language processing or some other area entirely? Just like medicine or engineering, sooner or later you need to choose a path that most fascinates you.

There are foundational elements that apply to whatever area you choose to specialise in. These consist of:

- Google have some excellent technical discussions, deeper level guides and opportunities to get hands-on with different facets of AI. As a number of the tools for AI used are developed by Google, they offer the chance to experiment with them on their Google Cloud, an excellent way to go deeper. As links get old very quickly, simply search for 'Google AI Education"

- Meta also offers exposure to AI concepts; they have more advanced as well as beginner resources and the white papers that they make available are very valuable and provide a great foundation for your AI studies.

- Hands-on experimentation. We have looked at front-end tools (where you have a user-friendly interface to interact with) but you are now going to go deeper. You need to start looking at core tools such as **TensorFlow**, **Keras** and **PyTorch.**

- Python is the scripting language of choice for a very large number of AI tools. Luckily it is one of the easier scripting languages to learn and it's, well, a scripting language. This means that unlike other languages, such as Java, which are compiled and can be very complex, Python is very straightforward to pick up.

- **PyTorch**, coming out of Meta's AI research arm, is a machine learning library,[42] incredibly useful for developing AI models focused on machine vision; however, can be applied to other areas as well such as natural language processing.

- **TensorFlow,** the big one. This is a one-stop shop (developed by Google) for you to build your own AI applications, experiment and use the huge libraries available.

- **Keras,** another Google tool, works closely with TensorFlow and provides a high-level neural network library, making Tensorflow easier to use. Great for getting started!

- **AI Other …** as you specialise you will find other tools that align with what you are trying to achieve. Such is the pace of AI development that you need to stay on top of new developments and tools.

- All of the tools cited have excellent learning resources on their respective websites and in addition to those

---

42 We don't mean a lot of books; we mean code that has already been developed that you can use yourself in whatever application you are building. It stops you from having to start from scratch, akin to having the foundations of your house already built and ready for you to do the rest.

don't forget to look at the YouTube learning options for each of them too. There are some excellent educators who break down implementation of these tools in a very clear and consistent manner.[43]

- Mathematics is key. As you know, algorithms are heavily mathematics focused, they rely on statistics, probability theory as well as core principles such as calculus. Brush up on these concepts as they will stand you in good stead as you go deeper.

- Get involved in AI forums, there are a ton out there, the logically named **AI Forums** is a solid place to start. It does focus a lot on AI dealmaking (naturally as that is huge) but also covers new developments and trends, a good place to start. Kaggle is another excellent resource, they cover all levels of machine learning and if you have a question, no matter how obscure, there is a good chance you will find an answer there.

  Finally, get out there. Is there any local machine learning, AI groups you can join? Online is good but nothing beats actually meeting a group of like-minded individuals.

[43] Codemy and Boris Meinardus are especially good creators that give excellent practical advice.

29: AI and Jobs – The Robots Are Coming ...

'Jobs don't disappear; they evolve. Deleting people from repetitive jobs frees them up to be more creative. The future of the human race is hedged on creativity.' – Gary Kasparov

One of the biggest concerns about AI is the impact on jobs. These fears are not unfounded but do need to be put into context. There will undoubtedly be jobs that will be lost due to AI. Some of the most likely to be impacted will be ones that have the following traits:

Tier 1: Skilled manual work – low risk of being replaced by AI

This tier of worker is one that must work in a specific environment and requires great manual dexterity as well as very specific skills, for example a hospital, factory or a care home.[44] These roles are the very last to be replaced as they require great manual skill and in the healthcare industry, they are not especially repetitive. The care that a nurse is required to give patients requires skills in medication, patient needs and physical skills, for example blood pressure or temperature readings. This is something that current AI-enabled robots struggle to do. Current medical robots are highly specialised, for example Leonardo surgical robots, while trials are ongoing with robots that can execute ultrasound tests and robots that can suture wounds.

As a result, the risk of replacement here is low, despite huge

---

[44] You may wonder about factories, aren't there a huge number of robots already in factories? Yes, especially in the manufacturing space for vehicles and high-risk environments.

demand for these skills, particularly in the West with rapidly ageing populations. However, it should be noted that there are more generalised AI-enabled robots being developed to execute a range of tasks in the medical field. Japan has led the world in this domain due to a demographic that is rapidly ageing where support for seniors is required.

More controversially roles such as truck driving are unlikely to be replaced by AI in the next five years. They are safety critical roles and the technology for self-driving vehicles **at the moment** is not at the stage where we can 100 per cent trust an AI system to manage all driving situations. What **is** likely is AI-assisted systems that reduce the workload on the driver and increase safety levels. It should be noted however that Tesla, Waymo and Aurora are all working on autonomous freight systems so beyond five years there is a possibility of replacement of drivers...

Tier 2: High knowledge/experience workers – medium risk of being replaced by AI

The key difference between AI and previous technology changes is the **commoditisation** of knowledge. Previously knowledge has been a scarce commodity, that is why your lawyer can charge you $1,000 an hour, their knowledge **is** the commodity. This is the result of years of law school, learned experience and expertise gained in the role. The same applies for roles in finance and medicine.

AI changes this. An AI lawyer can *in theory* instantly look up case law, provide explanations and support a client. The same applies for a doctor or a financial analyst. However, as we discussed in Chapter 20, generative AI systems have an alarming habit of making stuff up, or hallucinating. Hence, reliance on AI systems to completely take over these areas is unlikely.

What **is** likely is that in all of these fields, AI will greatly assist how they operate. Their skills will be augmented and importantly for company boards, so will the productivity of those using it.
Microsoft's Copilot (the AI tool embedded into their Edge browser and being rolled out across the 0365 Office suite) was found in a study to increase productivity for tasks such as meeting summarisation, email creation and other administrative tasks.

In addition, software developers benefit massively from AI support. An awful lot of code creation is not done from scratch, existing repositories or libraries, of standard commands and routines are reused. One of the most heavily used sources of this code is GitHub.

An AI-enabled version, GitHub Copilot, works with developers as they code, as the developer starts typing code the system autocompletes, pulling the relevant library to the task at hand. Copilot also learns what the developer is working on and anticipates code that they may need to use. It's very effective, some studies have shown that it increases code quality and output by up to 70 per cent. For experienced developers it makes a massive difference and for more junior developers it has been shown to boost their skills by aiding their learning and overall development.

Outside of software development, large language models trained for specific fields will be used to support key decisions and will focus on lower-level work, freeing this level of worker to put energy into specific higher-level decisions that require nuance, impact and an understanding of precedence and next steps.

Examples could be language models trained on a law firm's data, a consulting firm's data or an accounting firm's records. Remember that AI is exceptionally good at spotting patterns in data, if you are a law firm and have two million items of information for a large client that is part of the discovery process getting insight into this data, pulling out salient information based on your prompts (questions) is incredibly powerful.

More junior levels, however, will be at risk; for example, finance roles where an analyst is required to execute due diligence on publicly available information could be replaced by AI, feeding that information to a more senior individual.

The OpenAI company do estimate that the impact and risk of AI is likely to be three times more for higher paid than lower paid roles, but there is an element of nuance there.

There is an exception in knowledge workers, those who work in writing and editing. Following the release of ChatGPT there was a marked decline on freelance platforms of both jobs advertised and the rates paid for these jobs. While far from perfect, it was clear that the market decided that 'good enough' was enough for these roles. We explored this further in Chapter 25 where we looked at the impact on the entertainment industries.

Tier 3: Blend of repetitive and cognitive work – high risk of being replaced by AI

These are roles where the work has quite defined parameters. Call centre staff are a prime example of this. There is a core number of enquiries that are asked by customers on a regular basis, these are pretty well defined, as are the answers. These can and already are being responded to by chatbots (which are AI-enabled). The next stage is to deal with more complex queries, which again can be handled by AI systems. Only those call centre roles where empathy and specific cultural factors are required are likely to require human input.

Key things:

- Physical labour or work that requires mobility in any way is unlikely to be replaced by AI soon.
- Knowledge work jobs are likely to be under threat.
- Repetitive, path-oriented work is likely to be replaced by AI.
- Entirely new roles will be created by AI, ones that currently do not exist.

30: Wait, It's Not All Bad ...

'Some of the worst things in my life never happened.' – Mark Twain

Amidst all the doom surrounding AI, the fear of Terminator Mark II, millions of job losses and general disruption to our lives there is a need for some perspective. AI has the potential to change our lives massively; however, in very positive as well as negative ways. The area of building inclusive technologies for those who up until now have not been major beneficiaries of advances is clearly significant.

If we look at transportation, the exponential increases that we are seeing in autonomous vehicle systems opens a range of possibilities. Disabled Individuals with restricted movement suddenly have the opportunity for travel independence again, as their self-driving vehicle takes care of the drive, they no longer need to wait on specialised taxis or rely on someone to do the driving for them. Similarly, older drivers who are less confident in their driving abilities as they age no longer need to worry about the journey. They can simply tell their car where to go.

AI capabilities in image recognition have already been harnessed in new and quite wonderful ways. One company, signfordeaf, enables hearing-impaired individuals to have text automatically translated into sign language, the user clicks on a portion of text and the AI plugin instantly renders it into sign language. Even more impressive has been the work of the highly talented engineer Priyanjali Gupta and her AI model that translates sign

language instantly into English.[45] She used a pre-trained model based on American sign language and while at an early version the potential is huge.

AI as an enabler in medical discoveries means that drug combination testing, a process that can take years, can be massively accelerated, leading to new, very focused treatments for the ill. Iterative testing enables scientists to experiment with new options for component combinations, such as those used in battery design. One experiment conducted by the US Department of Energy's Laboratory on thirty-two million possible component combinations narrowed down the list to just eighteen in eighty hours.[46]

This was admittedly done using some serious computing hardware, part of what Microsoft call their Azure Quantum Elements service (a great name by the way) combined with an AI model. It shows what can be done as AI models become far more computing efficient, with the massive benefits to materials science, new drug discovery and more general engineering breakthroughs: aircraft design as one example.

But what about all those engineers and scientists? Won't they be put out of work? We explored the different tiers of work that will be impacted in the previous chapter, and there will undoubtedly be an impact on jobs of the future. Also, we can't deny that entire industries and jobs will be upended. However, as with any new technology, new jobs and skills will be created.

---

45 Read more about this remarkable engineer here: https://interestingengineering.com/innovation/ai-translates-asl-in-real-time

46 https://www.utilitydive.com/news/pnnl-microsoft-artificial-intelligence-research-battery/704176/#:~:text=%E2%80%9COur%20collaboration%20with%20Microsoft%20is,Science%20and%20Technology%20Tony%20Peurrung.

We started with prompt engineers but that is very early, roles such as data engineers, data model, language model experts will all likely proliferate along with roles that are yet to be devised.

In addition, what AI will do is free these professionals from the drudgery of what we shall call lower-order tasks. Such as researching which materials and which designs are the most optimal for the problem they are looking to solve. Instead, they will have a vastly narrower set of results or designs that give them an enormous head start in their research. In effect, they have their own Jarvis that works with them as they approach and solve new problems.

In the personal realm, having AI companions that can advise and assist us with our daily lives, such as planning trips, supporting our health and generally making our lives easier has to be positive, especially as populations in so many countries have older age profiles and will need more support as they age.

Key things:

- AI has the potential to positively impact the worlds of transportation, medical diagnostics and the way in which we work.
- Scientific discoveries are likely to be massively accelerated with AI as the ability to analyse and extract patterns from existing data plays to the strengths of AI.

31 AI: Limitations

While we have looked at work and how different professions will or won't be impacted by AI in the future, more research is now being done on the impact of generative AI on the way we work.

The noted and highly respected Google DeepMind researcher Nicholas Carlini, who has previously focused on vulnerabilities in large language models, has published research on what AI is good at and not so good at doing and his results shine a light on some of the limitations of what AI can and can't do.

What Carlini found was that AI models were excellent, for example, at creating code for a website showing an American flag that changed colour as the user clicked on it. However, it couldn't write the code to show a birthday cake that played a song at the same time. Similarly, ChatGPT-4 can create code to show a tic-tac-toe game and let you play the game. Yet, it struggles to identify a winning move in the same game.

This aligns with other research that shows that AI systems are so poor at basic mathematical questions that some researchers are calling it the 'math gap'. The inability to answer fairly standard high school math questions lies in the difference between pattern recognition and **reasoning**.

Show an AI system one million data elements and it can parse and identify patterns in the data incredibly quickly. Ask it to perform reasoning against that data and the answers are far less clear and more confused. The key challenge is that AI is great at distinguishing between cats and dogs, but ask it to then understand the meaning of 'pets' and it gets confused. This is reasoning, and humans are really good at this and AI systems are really quite poor at it.

Reasoning is challenging for AI systems and when you add in true understanding of mathematical problems and solutions it becomes even harder. AI training data may contain thousands of mathematical solutions to problems but the logic that links the solutions together, that a human can grasp and use to solve an entirely new math problem, frequently proves too much for AI models.

There are persuasive arguments that AI is really only a semantic parrot; that is, it simply regurgitates information that it has absorbed without understanding the true meaning or insight that it provides.

This then calls into question the very meaning of the term *artificial intelligence*; can we call it intelligent if it has no true understanding of what it produces? We risk falling into a philosophical debate on what it means to be intelligent but ultimately, whether the technology is intelligent does not change the fact that it is having a meaningful impact on many different fields.

It is for you to assess how it will impact you personally, hopefully armed with the knowledge from this book, from your own experimentation and further learning, you can chart a course that benefits you the most. Simply ignoring this technology is not an option; time to grab your board and surf that wave!

Key things:

- AI is great at many things but it still struggles with, what for a human are, pretty basic reasoning tasks.
- This is an area of AI that major language models are looking to improve. To reason is to be human and AI systems need to be able to do this.

Glossary: Key terms in artificial intelligence

- **Adversarial training**: the AI training process of pitting two kinds of neural networks, a generator and a discriminator, against each other in order to create the most accurate output.
- **Algorithm**: Think of these as rules for the computer to follow, for example, if you see this street sign you need to slow down.
- **Artificial intelligence (AI):** The Big One. The attempt to get computers to think and act like humans.
- **Augmented reality:** Overlaying what you can see with specific information. A heads-up display in a car shows you the speed you are travelling at while still letting you see the road ahead.
- **Autonomous**: A machine that can do something by itself, with no human input. Like a flying car that takes off and lands by itself, with slightly terrified passengers in the back as there's no pilot up front.
- **Bias**: This is a challenge in AI where an AI system will unfairly favour one element, category, group or individual over another. More comprehensive training data is part of the solution to this problem.
- **Big data**: The use of very large data sets that can be analysed by AI models to identify patterns and solutions to problems. Examples include weather data measurements, stock exchange movements or clinical trial data.
- **Binary classification**: The sorting of data by an AI model into two categories, useful for systems such as spam filters for your email.
- **Chatbot**: The quite annoying automated responses that you see and interact with on websites and apps. They

highlight how narrow AI can be annoying as once you stray out of a standard set of questions; they get very confused very quickly.

- **ChatGPT:** Chat generative pre-trained transformer**.** The AI tool developed by OpenAI that takes prompts from a user and returns text.
- **Chat prompt:** The phrasing of commands used in AI prompt tools such as ChatGPT.
- **Classification**: When we are using machine learning to classify or place a piece of data into a specific category. This could be code, text, an image or a sound. For example, as part of the machine learning process we train the (visual) system on lots of pictures of ducks. As it has learned on lots of pictures of ducks and classifies them into the category ducks or wild birds, the next time the system comes across a duck it knows it's a duck.
- **Computer vision:** This is how we teach computers to see and understand images and videos, like recognising a cat in a picture.
- **Copilot:** Generative AI system developed by the Microsoft Corporation.
- **DALL-**E: An AGI company that lets users create images from prompts.
- **Data**: All the elements that a computer needs to use to create models of how the world works.
- **Data cleansing**: There is a term in computing, ***garbage in, garbage out***. When you are putting together training data (like lots of pictures of ducks) you want to make sure you don't have random pictures of non-ducks in there. Data cleansing attempts to do this by for example taking out any pictures of eagles or peacocks from your duck training data.
- **Data mining**: This is like panning for a gold in a huge riverbed. AI systems are trained to spot patterns in data that could herald new insights that a human couldn't

possibly do due to the sheer amount of data. Hence the term data mining.

- **Deep learning**: This is a type of machine learning that copies how the human brain works. It uses something called neural networks to learn from lots of data.
- **Dimensionality reduction**: No, not a rock band, but it would make a great name. This is taking a lot of data and stripping out all the unnecessary elements while preserving the core. Tesla does this with their vision data from their cars, they don't need the background images that lead to the car taking avoiding action, they need the car to focus on the most important elements such as a swerving car or a road sign.
- **DYOR:** Do your own research. Don't assume that your AI companion is correct 100 per cent of the time. Check multiple sources and don't be like the lawyer who relied on AI to research case law, which then proceeded to make up a ton of totally fictitious cases. The presiding judge was *not* happy ...
- **Ensemble system learning:** Ensemble system learning, from the French for *together,* is a process that combines more than one AI learning algorithm together to get improved results. This reduces bias and reduces, though doesn't completely prevent, hallucinations.
- **Edge computing:** The process of moving data manipulation away from large cloud-hosted systems and towards 'on device' computing. For example, executing tasks on your cell phone itself without the cell phone needing to send data anywhere for processing.
- **Generative AI:** The ability to create text, images, sounds and more using artificial intelligence systems or programs.
- **Hallucinations:** The tendency for AI systems to just make random stuff up. Don't forget to DYOR (do your own research).
- ***I, Robot*:** A really great movie that gives a great example of the three laws rule for robots, invented by the

science fiction author Isaac Asimov and starting to gain adoption in the robotic community (the three laws bit, not the killer robots bits). See *Three Laws* in this glossary further down for what the laws consist of.

- **Internet of Things (IoT)**: Connecting many devices together and enabling them to connect to the wider internet. Think of connected fridges and the other smart devices in your home that can gather and share data.
- **Labels:** A super important term in AI, training data needs to be labelled correctly, our images of ducks need to be clearly labelled as that makes classification more accurate.
- **Llama: Llama** and **Llama2** stand for large language model meta-AI. These have been released to researchers for AI research and have been trained on more than one trillion tokens according to Meta.
- **LLM:** Large language model – A form of AI that can create and recognise text, speech, images and more. All based on machine learning that is trained on huge data sets.
- **Machine learning**: This is a branch of AI that looks to create models that can learn from data rather than being programmed specifically to do something.
- **Midjourney:** An AGI company that specialises in creating images from prompts. Operates a paid for model (although sometimes offers free trials). In close competition with the likes of Stability AI's Stable Diffusion and OpenAI's DALL-E.
- **Model**: School's done; my brain is full. [47]Once training has been completed you have a model that is used by the AI system, think of it as the AI's brain.
- **Natural language generation (NLG)**: The process of taking unstructured data and using it to create output that is readable by humans. One example would be

[47] With thanks to Gary Larson, see his Far Side cartoon here: https://slideplayer.com/slide/8372499/

taking thousands of data measurements such as air pressure, humidity and precipitation and creating a weather forecast.

- **Natural language processing (NLP):** Teaching computers how to understand the patterns and flows of human language, this is key to predicting the next word or words in a sentence.
- **Neural network**: The art and skill of recognising patterns, just as the human brain does, by labelling data and extensive training on very large data sets.
- **Nvidia**: Enormous chipmaking company, founded in 1993, that specialises not only in making very high-end AI chips, called RTX GPUs but also develop systems and software that are designed for large language models. They also make cool gaming chips. See the chapter on them for more detail.
- **OpenAI:** The company that developed ChatGPT. One of the pioneers of generative AI. See the chapter on OpenAI for more information.
- **Overfitting**: Think of the clever kid in class who has practised for today's test by studying all the past exam papers and acing those tests. Then, on the day of the exam she is presented with a question that she hasn't seen before and is stumped. With AI, instead of seeing a pattern in the data it is fed it instead memorises the exact answers so can't cope with new and different data. This is a real problem with AI systems and is partially to blame for hallucinations.
- **Patterns**: A part of training AI systems is to train on known patterns, for example if these fifteen inputs all occur, such as temperature is x, humidity is y, then there is a strong probability that it will snow tomorrow. This feeds into predictions, see below.
- **Prediction:** Key to AI systems, the ability to predict the next word in a sentence or for example to make a judgment on what the weather will be like next

Tuesday, based on the patterns that it has been trained on.

- **Regression analysis:** A form of supervised learning where you have both the inputs (e.g. temperature, humidity, precipitation, air pressure) and outputs (probability of snowfall in the next eight hours). If this is done correctly the AI algorithm will detect a **pattern** and when presented with different inputs it will give an output (will it snow or not?) based on the known patterns (e.g. there is an 80% probability it will snow in the next eight hours).
- **Reinforcement learning:** How you get better at playing Space Invaders, you know not to do stuff as you keep getting blasted away. After a few goes you usually get better at it, through trial and error. That how AI systems work, although they learn **a lot** faster than you and I do.
- **Robotics**: An area where we blend AI with robots, to give us machines that can operate autonomously or controlled.
- **Supervised learning:** In training the AI model (machine learning) we start off with clearly labelled data. We tell the machine learning model, 'Here are one hundred pictures of dogs, each of these images is a dog.' This is the first step, the next one is semi-supervised learning:
- **Semi-supervised learning:** This time we might label twenty of the pictures as dogs, the remaining eighty pictures might be dogs, might not be dogs. The ML needs to figure it out. Once completed we then go to the final stage.
- **Sources:** When you need to check specific facts that AI has produced, double-check using one or more search engines. These are a more reliable source of information and while they may display bias, they are far less likely to make facts up.
- **The three laws of robotics:** First devised by the science fiction author Isaac Asimov.
  1. A robot may not injure a human being or, through

inaction, allow a human being to come to harm.
2. A robot must obey orders given it by human beings except where such orders would conflict with the first law.
3. A robot must protect its own existence as long as such protection does not conflict with the first or second law.

- **Unsupervised learning:** Flying solo, we need you to identify all the dogs in this unlabelled collection of one hundred images. There might be one hundred dogs, there may be none. See if you can figure it out.
- **Underfitting:** This is where the machine learning system (ML) doesn't have enough data, or the data itself is not good enough to teach the system to recognise patterns.
- **Training:** This is when we teach the computer to do something, like recognising a cat in a picture. We do this by giving it **lots** of examples (data). It appears that most ML training projects use data sets that have at least one hundred million records and some are way larger than this.

Further Research

There are a huge amount of resources, both online and in book format, to further your knowledge. The largest companies innovating in artificial intelligence have excellent resources that are generally free and updated on a very frequent basis so take time to check out Google, MetaLabs, OpenAI and Microsoft's resources.

For true visionaries in this space and ones who can guide us to where we could go have a look at the following:

Ray Kurzweil: The ultimate AI futurist, his most recent book, *The Singularity Is Nearer*, has some interesting predictions of how we will merge with computers.

Michio Kaku: A visionary who has focused deeply on quantum computing and the implications for AI.

Nick Bostrom: Author of *Superintelligence*, groundbreaking work on where AI could take us.

Kate Darling: Pioneer on the links between AI and robotics.

Tom Taulli: Great on the underlying concepts behind AI.

Some excellent books and scientific articles worth examining. Remember the pace of change is remarkable so checking for updates is key.

Books:

- **AI 2041: Ten Visions for Our Future** by Chen Qiufan & Kai-Fu Lee: A blend of science fiction and analysis exploring AI's impact by 2041.

- **Atlas of AI: Power, Politics, and the Planetary Costs of Artificial Intelligence** by Kate Crawford: Examines the broader implications of AI development.

- **Artificial Intelligence: A Modern Approach** by Peter Norvig & Stuart Russell: A comprehensive textbook on AI theories and applications.

- **The Master Algorithm: How the Quest for the Ultimate Learning Machine Will Remake Our World** by Pedro Domingos: Discusses the search for a 'master' machine learning algorithm.

- **Superintelligence: Paths, Dangers, Strategies** by Nick Bostrom: Explores the future of AI and its potential risks.

- **Artificial Intelligence For Dummies (2nd Edition)** by Luca Massaron, John Mueller: An introduction to AI for beginners.

- **Artificial Intelligence Basics: A Non-Technical Introduction** by Tom Taulli: Explains AI's societal impact and future implications

- **Python: Beginner's Guide to Artificial Intelligence** by Denis Rothman, Matthew Lamons, Rahul Kumar: Teaches AI development using Python.

Scientific Articles:

- **Chatbots Struggle to Answer Medical Questions in Widely Spoken Languages**: Discusses the limitations of chatbots in providing medical information.

- **Inside the Race to Protect Artists from Artificial Intelligence**: Covers AI-generated art and its ethical issues.

- **What Google's New AI Fruit Fly Can Teach Us about Real Behavior**: Explores an AI that learned from observing real insects.

- **Can AI Replace Human Research Participants? These Scientists See Risks**: Looks at the potential risks of using AI to generate research data.

- **How Artificial Intelligence Helped Write This Award-Winning Song**: Describes how AI algorithms assist in creating music.

- **God Chatbots Offer Spiritual Insights on Demand. What Could Go Wrong?**: Examines the use of AI in providing religious guidance.

- **Inside the AI Competition That Decoded an Ancient Herculaneum Scroll**: Details how AI helped read scrolls preserved by a volcanic eruption.

- **Building Intelligent Machines Helps Us Learn How Our Brain Works**: Discusses insights into human intelligence through AI design.

- **Too Much Trust in AI Poses Unexpected Threats to the Scientific Process**: Warns against over-reliance on AI in scientific research.

Online Courses, these are foundation levels and you can go as complex as you like. All should be available for free on YouTube or via the respective institutions online course sites. MIT is the big one here, source of huge amounts of information!

MIT

- **AI 101**: **An introduction to artificial intelligence** designed for those with little to no background in the subject, covering key concepts and interactive exercises. MIT has one of the most comprehensive set of lectures available on AI, amazing that so much of it is available and free to watch!

Harvard:

- **CS50's Introduction to Artificial Intelligence with Python**: Teaches machine learning in Python, covering graph search algorithms, classification, optimization. Really excellent.

Yale:

- **Artificial Intelligence:** A study of the practice of building systems that can solve complex tasks traditionally requiring human intelligence. Good intro to theories that underpin AI.

Cambridge:

- **Artificial Intelligence and Us**: Provides an understanding of AI, its benefits, challenges, ethical concerns, and impact on society. Big picture stuff here, very insightful if at times alarming!

Thank you so much for reading *AI in 8 Minutes*. I hope you enjoyed reading the book as much as I enjoyed researching and writing it. If you did enjoy the book and have the time and inclination, please consider writing a review on the book's Amazon page.

Thank you!

David Bruce

Ai
IN
8 MINUTES

Made in the USA
Monee, IL
04 November 2026

67384440R00079